Preachı
for Special
Services

Other books by Scott M. Gibson

The Big Idea of Biblical Preaching (co-editor)
Making a Difference in Preaching (editor)
A. J. Gordon: American Premillennialist (author)

Preaching *for* Special Services

SCOTT M. GIBSON

Baker Books
A Division of Baker Book House Co
Grand Rapids, Michigan 49516

© 2001 by Scott M. Gibson

Published by Baker Books
a division of Baker Book House Company
P.O. Box 6287, Grand Rapids, MI 49516-6287

Printed in the United States of America

Library of Congress Cataloging-in-Publication Data

Gibson, Scott M., 1957-
    Preaching for special services / Scott M. Gibson.
      p.   cm.
    Includes bibliographical references.
    ISBN 0–8010–9111–X
    1. Preaching. 2. Occasional services. I. Title.
    BV4221.G53   2001
    251'.1—dc21   2001025034

For current information about all releases from Baker Book House, visit our web site:
                  http://www.bakerbooks.com

In memory of
Dr. Gwyn Walters

Contents

Foreword

This book is written for pastors or those planning to be pastors. Let me state the obvious. Only pastors have congregations. Lawyers have clients who consult them when they face lawsuits and physicians have patients who schedule appointments for yearly physicals. But pastors have congregations.

Ministers stand before their congregations on most Sundays, of course, to deliver their word from God. But they do much more than that. They get bound up in their people's lives. If pastors stay with their churches for several years, they will witness and experience the struggles and celebrations of people who make up their church families. Children are born into the congregation, the converted get baptized into it, and couples get married standing before it. The minister is there. He is expected to say something significant. Ministers also stand in dimly lit hospital rooms to whisper assurance to those in the darkening hours of life, and then a day or two later they must stand and speak words of strength and comfort to those in their congregations who are left behind.

Scott Gibson and other writers refer to these times as "special occasions." That sounds a bit cold and impersonal. These "special occasions" actually make up the stuff of life. They are the moments when a minister grieves with those who grieve or laughs heartily with those who laugh. On these occasions, he searches for words from the Word to make sense of what seems senseless or finds other words to take happy times and fill them with deeper joy.

Yet, what does a pastor say? What should a pastor do? Any thoughtful minister wonders how to make the most of these important—and often unexpected—moments when eternal truth must speak to human pain or celebration. How do we weep with those who weep or laugh with those who laugh? What have others done in the past? What can we do now? All of us have to speak more often than we should. We need all the help we can get to make the most of our congregation's special occasions.

Scott Gibson cares about pastors and the people they care about. That is why he wrote this book—to give pastors some direction on what to say and do when they speak to the sad and glad experiences of members in their congregations. Fledgling pastors and even experienced ministers will profit from this little volume. Beginners can "learn and live" (which is much easier than having to "live and learn"), and those who are farther along will find themselves reading and saying, "Yes, of course, that's right. I wish I had read this years ago!"

Haddon W. Robinson

Acknowledgments

Books are not written in isolation: Authors need help, and I have received help from many. First, thanks to the trustees of Gordon-Conwell Theological Seminary and to president Dr. Walter C. Kaiser Jr. for the opportunity to write this book while on sabbatical study leave, which they graciously granted to me for the fall of 1999.

I am grateful to my friend and mentor Dean Kenneth L. Swetland, the members of the Division of the Ministry of the Church, and the Faculty Personnel and Policy Committee of Gordon-Conwell Theological Seminary for helping me prepare for sabbatical study and for supporting me in the project.

Thanks to all my students in my preaching classes, especially those in the "Preaching for Special Occasions" course over the years. Their fingerprints are found everywhere in this book.

Deepest thanks to one of my boys, Thomas V. Haugen, and his wife, Lauri, for the gracious way they put me up—and put up with me—while I wrote and researched in Edin-

~ 11 ~

burgh, Scotland. Thanks, Tom, for reading the manuscript in its early stages.

Thanks also to Patrick I. Lowthian who read some of the manuscript and even tested the material on a couple of sermons. Thanks, my boy.

Thanks to David Forsythe who read the entire manuscript. I know you are a busy pastor, David. I appreciate your insights and comments.

Thanks to Dr. Paul Fiddes and the tutors and staff at Regent's Park College, University of Oxford, for accommodating me while I wrote and researched there.

Thanks to Paul Harris and Karen Smith for hosting me in Neath, Wales, and to Nigel J. Robb for the study visit to the University of Aberdeen, Scotland.

A mountain of thanks to Kerry L. Bender, my skilled student Byington research assistant, for his help in putting together this book. Thanks, my boy. My previous Byington research assistants also deserve mention as they helped me by combing through journals and periodicals: Stephen J. Sebastian, Michael Laird, Boo Arnold, Stephen Lane, and Glen L. Massey.

A special word of thanks to Todd M. Smedley, my chapel assistant, who guarded my time during my sabbatical. He took telephone calls, dealt with questions, defended my door, and gave me encouragement. Thanks, my boy.

Thanks also to Dianne Newhall, my able secretary, who held down the fort during my sabbatical. Thanks for marching into the battle for me, Lady Di.

I am grateful to my colleague, mentor, and friend, Dr. Haddon W. Robinson, for his willingness to read the manuscript, for his invaluable comments, and for writing the foreword to this book. Learning Haddon Robinson's central-idea philosophy of preaching has revolutionized my preaching, and teaching men and women the skills for preaching has been a thrill for me. Thanks, Haddon, for your friendship and for the privilege of working with you. It has been a dream come true.

Thanks to my family and especially to Rhonda, my wife, for prayers, support, and encouragement. Your expressions of care mean more than you will ever know.

Finally, many thanks to Donald Stephenson, my editor at Baker Book House. I appreciate your help, insight, encouragement, and patience. I am also thankful for the assistance from Baker Book House staff. They have been great.

I dedicate this book to the memory of Dr. Gwyn Walters, former professor of preaching at Gordon-Conwell Theological Seminary, who died in 1992. I was a student of Dr. Walters when I attended Gordon-Conwell for the master of divinity degree. He invested a lot in me over the years and for that I am grateful. Because of Dr. Walters's interest in my life direction, I followed him as a teacher of preaching at Gordon-Conwell, but his shoes are far too big for me to fill. I remain his student; he will always be my teacher.

1

Preaching
for Special Services

*Special occasions call for skillful planning. Like the poor,
they are ever with us, and their number bids fair to increase.*

Andrew W. Blackwood

An almost endless parade of potential special occasions confronts a preacher. Some come from the church year such as Advent and Christmas, Epiphany and Lent, then Easter and Pentecost. In addition to the church year are national holidays, as religiously oriented as Thanksgiving, as politically potent as the Fourth of July, or as sentimental as Mother's Day or Father's Day.

Other holidays are promoted by the greeting card industry: Secretary's Day, Grandparent's Day, or even Groundhog Day. It seems that the list of new "holy-days" grows each year. On top of all of this, there are the special days established by the denomination—any number of missionary Sundays, retired ministers' Sundays, Sundays for special offerings, and more. The chorus of voices vying for the spotlight on Sundays can be bewildering for the pastor as he or she intends to preach biblical messages to nourish the congregation during the course of a year.

Some pastors succumb to these extraneous demands because they do not plan well. Their sermons are not prepared in advance and therefore these pastors welcome anything that will fill the time on Sunday morning—and there are enough special interests to take up every Sunday of the year.

The key to a healthy preaching diet—for a preacher and the congregation—is to plan well ahead of time, carving out a schedule that will take into consideration the spiritual maturity and needs of the church. When this is done, then and only then will the preacher be able to filter through various special Sundays.[1]

The preaching plan a pastor develops will serve the preacher and the congregation well. Certain holidays may be recognized as the special focus in the sermon or mentioned in prayer or given attention in another part of the worship service.[2]

While church-year, national, greeting-card, and denominational special days are important, they are not the focus of this book. Instead we will concentrate on the preparation of sermons for a fifth category of special occasions, which includes baptisms or infant presentations, the Lord's Supper, funerals, weddings, and evangelistic emphasis.

The thrust of this book is not the entire special-occasion worship service but more specifically, the special-occasion sermon. There are helpful books that assist the pastor in creating a meaningful worship experience for the congregation, especially for baptisms, weddings, the Lord's Supper, and funerals. However, there are few resources that speak directly to the development of the sermon for special occasions.

Why Special-Occasion Preaching?

Our focus, then, is those sermons designed for occasions largely outside the ordinary preaching schedule.[3] There are factors associated with special-occasion preaching that may not relate to the preacher's regular weekly preaching schedule. Perhaps the prevailing question that confronts the preacher is, Why special-occasion preaching? The answer to this question is: Preaching at these times allows the preacher to speak the Word of God to those gathered, to round out the worship, to bring focus to the occasion.

A good biblical theology affirms that the preaching of the Word is worship. In these special-occasion services the Word is to be preached.[4] Most of the special occasions dealt with in this book have a liturgy, a series of readings and prayers associated with them. Our task as preachers is to complement the liturgy and speak God's Word on the special occasion, making it a total worship experience.

Of course, some special occasions, like a funeral, come with little warning. Still, ministers are to "preach the Word" by being "prepared in season and out of season." In addition, they "correct, rebuke and encourage—with great patience and careful instruction" (2 Tim. 4:2). Special-occasion preaching is not to be treated lightly. As one preacher says, "A special occasion sermon is not a way of pandering to jaded palates or a ploy to catch people out at a moment of vulnerability." He continues, "A special occasion sermon is a word fitly spoken."[5]

Exegetical preachers have both biblical and theological commitments. Carl E. Braaten put it this way: "Believing and thinking belong together in both preaching and theologizing." Another theologian said, "Theology without preaching is empty and preaching without theology is blind."[6]

British pastor D. W. Cleverley Ford urges preachers to make a determined effort to have the special occasion and the sermon teem with significance. Ford writes:

> The preacher's responsibility . . . is to try and make the special occasion take on special significance, so much so that some person present may perhaps confess after the passage of years, "How my life has changed! And how much is due to that special occasion which I can never forget. Something happened for me which altered my perspectives."[7]

Michael Courtney reflects on the power of the funeral worship service in his life after his baby died and how the Word preached brought comfort and hope:

> Worship services have many functions in a time of crisis. This service saved our faith. It allowed us and others to mourn our losses. It reminded us that God is love when there was so much to suggest otherwise. It allowed our brothers and sisters a way to say they were sorry and that they cared during a situation unfamiliar and uncomfortable to them. It gave us the opportunity to worship God when we desperately needed to do so.[8]

The purpose of any special-occasion sermon is to give a clear, listener-sensitive, biblically based word to men and women who are sometimes eager and often desperate to hear it.

The Design of the Book

Each of the succeeding chapters will be shaped in the following way. First, I will provide the history of the sermon in the given special occasion. We will discover that some special-occasion preaching has more historical evidence or development than others. Next, I will examine the theology of preaching at the special occasion. A major section on the development of the sermon will serve as the centerpiece of the chapter. This will be followed by a discussion of the actual preaching of the sermon, an exercise to help the reader put into practice the principles set forth in the chapter, and a bibliography of resources.

The approach to sermon construction advocated in this book is based on Haddon W. Robinson's central-idea preaching.[9] Robinson's *Biblical Preaching* develops the step-by-step process of sermon construction, which teaches preachers to form sermons with a central—big—idea derived from the biblical text and communicated clearly to the listeners.[10] Haddon Robinson's approach to preaching is more than a method, it is a philosophy based on rhetorical principles and biblical exegesis.[11] The careful reader will read *Biblical Preaching* along with this book.

Sermons are rooted in the biblical text. They develop out of an understanding of what the biblical author intended to convey to the biblical readers. The preacher is to be aware of the biblical context, that is, the place in which the text to be preached fits into the flow of the author's writing and thought. In addition, the preacher wants to be conscious of the historical context. Then the preacher is ready to ask two questions of the biblical text to determine the idea of the passage as it fits into the larger context of the author's writing. The first is the subject question: What is the author talking about? For example, Why does Paul thank God for the Thessalonian Christians? The subject question uses any one of the interrogatives: who, what, when, where, why, and how. The context of the passage will determine which interrogative the preacher will use.

The subject question is followed by the complement answer. The complement answer completes the subject question. The complement answer to the sample subject question is, They have been models of faith, and people everywhere have heard about them.

The next step is to put the two—the subject question and the complement answer—together into a single, indicative statement. This step may be likened to homiletical mathematics: S + C = I. The interrogative form is deleted and the subject question and complement answer are combined into an indicative statement: Paul thanks God for the Thessalonian Christians because they have been models of faith and people everywhere have heard about them. There you have it, the central idea or exegetical idea of the passage. Following the determination of the exegetical idea, the preacher develops the homiletical idea. This is the preaching idea that captures the essence of the exegetical idea but is stated in a memorable way. The homiletical idea serves as the central idea and is key to Robinson's approach to preaching and therefore to special-occasion preaching.[12]

Each chapter in this book will deal with how one takes the biblical/homiletical idea and fashions a sermon for the specific occasion.

Clarity in Preaching

Clarity is a law for preaching.[13] The preacher should be clear about what the biblical text says, clear about who the listeners are, clear about the occasion, and clear about what he or she is going to say. If he or she is not clear about these things, there is likely to be homiletical homicide, or worse, suicide. Listeners will not know what the preacher said or even meant to say.

First, preachers must be clear about the biblical text. If preachers follow Robinson's steps discussed above about discovering the idea of the text, they will be clear. In the following chapters we will discuss how to become more comfortable in developing clarity when working with the text. Second, preachers must be clear about the listeners. The preacher must make every effort to know their needs, emotional state, age, and concerns. This helps a pastor communicate a sermon that will touch the listener while remaining faithful to the biblical text. Hughes Oliphant Old observes in his history of preaching, "It is of the essence of expository preaching that one interprets the needs and concerns of the congregation just as one interprets the Scriptures."[14]

Third, preachers must be clear about the occasion at which they are preaching. All occasions are special, and all occasions are different. A funeral may be conducted for an elderly woman or for a teenage boy. The wedding may be the joining of two college graduates or a nursing home couple. The preacher who is aware of these differences will be able to make the event more meaningful and biblical.

Fourth, preachers must be clear about what they will say. After taking into account the text, the audience, and the occasion, a sermon should be written out as a manuscript in a conversational style but not memorized.

The Preacher and Special Occasions

When pastors officiate at weddings, conduct a funeral, baptize an infant or believer, and even celebrate the Supper, they are not the focal point of the event. At a wedding the bride and groom are the featured participants. The funeral puts the deceased and the grieving family center-stage. The infant or confessing believer is the one celebrated at baptism. The Lord's death is remembered in the bread and the wine. Rarely will anyone remember that it was you who performed Thomas and Lauri's wedding. Nor will you be remembered for conducting the funeral of Alice Keihl.

Scarcely will anyone recall that you baptized Emerson Reichart. And you should not come to mind when the celebration of the Supper is remembered. The preacher is in the shadows.

Ultimately, God is at the center. We preach not that we will be remembered, but that God will be at the forefront in our preaching, and in the thinking, and in the living of those who gather. Eugene Peterson observes:

> Even when unnoticed, we are usually sure our presence makes a difference, sometimes a critical difference, for we have climbed to the abandoned places, the bereft lives, the "gaps" that Ezekiel wrote of (22:30), and have spoken Christ's Word and witnessed Christ's mercy.[15]

Søren Kierkegaard suggested that many people consider worship to be a drama in which God is the prompter, the minister is the actor, and the congregation is the audience. But Kierkegaard says that genuine worship is much different. Instead, the members of the congregation are the actors, the pastor is the prompter, and God is the audience.[16] Our commitment is to honor God through God-centered, Christ-centered preaching on special occasions that will make a difference in the listeners' lives.

Getting the Idea _____

1. What are the five groupings of special occasions discussed in this chapter?
2. What is the value of establishing a preaching plan as it relates to special occasions?
3. How would you answer the question, Why special-occasion preaching?

4. What is the philosophy of central-idea preaching?
   Name and discuss the steps to developing an idea.
5. What are the ways in which a biblical preacher wants
   to be clear?

Shelf-Wise

Gibson, Scott M., ed. *Making a Difference in Preaching: Haddon W. Robinson on Biblical Preaching.* Grand Rapids: Baker, 1999.

Robinson, Haddon W. *Biblical Preaching: The Development and Delivery of Expository Messages.* Grand Rapids: Baker, 1980.

Robinson, Haddon W. *Biblical Sermons: How Twelve Preachers Apply the Principles of Biblical Preaching.* Grand Rapids: Baker, 1989.

Schlafer, David J. *What Makes This Day Different? Preaching Grace on Special Occasions.* Boston: Cowley, 1998.

Willhite, Keith, and Scott M. Gibson, eds. *The Big Idea of Biblical Preaching: Connecting the Bible to People.* Grand Rapids: Baker, 1998.

2

Wedding Sermons

A wedding sermon, whenever it is included in a Christian marriage ceremony, provides a pastor with unique opportunities.

Francis C. Rossow

Some preachers sheepishly confess that they would rather conduct a funeral than a wedding. I can understand how they feel. One preacher lamented, "Weddings often seem like more trouble than they are worth."[1] There seem to be more uncontrollable variables associated with matrimonial celebrations than with most funerals. Although they are difficult, I cannot say that there has been one wedding that I have not enjoyed. I smile when I think of every one of them.

Since I no longer serve as a pastor at a local church, I tie fewer knots now, but the ceremonies over which I do officiate continue to be memorable. One summer I was involved in three weddings. They turned out to be the highlights of my summer. The first was my niece's. We are a close family and it was presumed that Uncle Scott would do the ceremony. I have celebrated dozens of marriages with scores of couples, but this one was different. She was my niece. People cry at weddings for all different kinds of reasons and I was not sure that I would not be among those who cried—with joy of course.

Not long before the ceremony my sister Jeanine, the bride's mother, said, "Are you going to be able to make it?" "Of course," I said. However, the way I answered her was not confident. I knew it, and I think she knew it too.

The processional began. My brother-in-law walked down the aisle with Jessica on his arm. He was proud. He was sad. He was joyful. He was crying. I could hardly look at him, but I had to. I had to be strong. I welcomed the congregation and gave the introductory statement. Then, with a quiver in my voice, I asked, "Who gives this woman to be married to this man?" Dan replied with more weepy vibrato, "Her mother and I." He sat down. There ended the first wave of emotion, but they kept coming throughout the ceremony like endless tides, even when I preached. The couple marched down the aisle and I slipped into the recesses of the pastor's study and thanked God for the special day.

For most pastors, weddings do not happen weekly. One pastor finds performing marriages a vital part of his ministry. He performs fifteen to twenty ceremonies a month.[2] For the rest of us fifteen to twenty marriages a year may seem high. Whatever the number, each one is different. Each one is special.

One of the ways to make a wedding different is to make the sermon significant. Someone may ask, however, "Why is a sermon included in the ceremony anyway?"

The History of the Wedding Sermon

Not all weddings include a sermon. Some consist of only the typical liturgical elements of vows, prayers, and pronouncement. Although the rituals for marriage ceremonies in some denominations do not formally include a place for the wedding sermon, there appear to be none that prohibit it.[3] David J. Schlafer says some have "believed that because these occasions are *so* personal, grace can better be mediated solely through the time-honored words of the traditional service."[4]

Yet a word fitly spoken can add to the wedding ceremony and be meaningful to the couple and the congregation. There is evidence of a long tradition of sermons or speeches at weddings.

Jewish marriage ceremonies can be charted at least to the Talmudic period.[5] In the first century, homilies were given in the synagogues on Sabbaths and at festivals, including weddings. After the fifth century, sermons in general declined.[6] We find sermons at weddings to be more common from the medieval period on. Preaching took place at the synagogue or at the wedding feast. The preacher was the groom, the father of the groom, or the father of the bride.[7]

Greek and Roman wedding speeches were influenced by poets, playwrights, rhetoricians, and Jewish marriage rites.[8] The early church father Origen of Alexandria (185–254) recognized the Jewish influence on Roman and Greek marriage rites. In his first sermon on the Song of Songs he observed:

> These are the characters in this book, which is at once a drama and a marriage song. And it is from this book that the heathen appropriated the epithalamium, and here is the source of this type of poem; for it is obviously a marriage-song that we have in the Song of Songs.[9]

The Roman and Greek epithalamium was a marriage poem.[10] Ambrose of Milan (339–397) was aware of the use of the epithalamium in early Christian weddings.[11] The epithalamium was a familiar literary form in classical antiquity used to invoke the goddess of love and featured erotic banter. The early church changed the practice. Paulinus of Nola (ca. 355–431) gave an epithalamium on the occasion of the wedding of Julian of Eclanum and his bride Titia (ca. 405). Instead of the usual sexual jesting, Paulinus focused on the Christian nature of marriage. He used the form of the poets but changed the content.[12]

By the fourth century a marriage liturgy was formed in both the East and the West that included the blessing of a bishop or priest.[13] Caesarius, Bishop of Arles (ca. 500–550), quoted in his sermons from marriage orations and emphasized the importance that couples receive the nuptial blessing.[14]

The marriage ceremony at a church building became obligatory in the eleventh century. The priest presided with witnesses looking on. Earlier the service took place near the church building. Eventually the ceremony was held at the church door with the priest blessing the marriage. By the twelfth century the church wedding ceremony was fully established inside the church with the priest pronouncing blessings.[15]

Both Martin Luther (1483–1546) and John Calvin (1509–1564) saw marriage as the responsibility of the government, not the church.[16] Luther preached at weddings, which was his chief contribution to the change in the liturgy.[17] John Knox (1505–1572) also preached at weddings and had "the parties assemble at the beginning of the sermon." He then began the ceremony "at tyme convenient."[18] Cranmer's wedding service was influenced by Luther and included a homily.[19]

Some seventeenth-century English wedding sermons lasted as long as an hour—or more. An example is one that Jeremy Taylor (1613–1667) preached, "The Marriage Ring."[20] Another sermon "preached in the Church of B. in

S. at the solemnization of a Marriage, had betweene W. B. and E. S. the Daughter of I. S. of London, Merchant" was based on Ezra 9:14, "Should wee returne to breake they Commandments, and to joyne in Marriage and affinitie with people of abominations?" The preacher's sermon, more than an hour long, told the couple to be aware of the "hatefull company and hellish condition" of the world.[21] The sermon John Donne (1573–1631) preached at the marriage of Mistress Margaret Washington at the Church of St. Clement Danes, May 30, 1621, titled "Preached at a Mariage," was also characteristically long and picked up numerous wedding themes.[22]

English Puritans placed the sermon or "exhortation" at the beginning of the liturgy.[23] Scottish Puritan services also included a sermon, which followed a prayer of confession and petition for God's blessing on the couple.[24] American Puritan Cotton Mather (1663–1728) wrote that a pastor "was usually employed, and a *Sermon* also preached on this Occasion."[25]

Eighteenth-century British Dissenters suffered under the Marriage Act of 1754, which did not allow marriages to be celebrated in any Dissenting chapel. Although the Act was not repealed until 1836, many Dissenters continued marriage services. The Baptist marriage service included vows followed by the sermon.[26]

In the nineteenth century, as is often the case today in countries where there are both civil and church ceremonies, the wedding sermon served as "the sealing and consecration of the civil wedding already contracted."[27] English Methodists included an "exhortation" in their wedding services.[28]

The wedding sermon has become part of many twentieth- and twenty-first-century ceremonies.[29] Among some of the more unusual wedding sermons or occasions is a sermon Dietrich Bonhoeffer (1906–1945) wrote in May 1943, "A Wedding Sermon from a Prison Cell."[30]

The wedding sermon has been shaped by rhetoric and by religious tradition and remains an important part of many services providing an opportunity for the couple and the congregation to hear a clear word from God. Some ministers try "to convince the couple not to interrupt a beautiful ceremony with a sermon,"[31] but preaching is important to wedding celebrations.

The Theology of Wedding Sermons

The wedding sermon serves as a window to understanding God's design for marriage. It provides the opportunity to help the couple and the congregation discern the meaning of marriage and to speak about what marriage looks like in the context of the church and its vision of God.

Marriage involves not just two people, but three: husband, wife, and God.[32] There exists a mysterious, invisible oneness in the couple: "The two will become one flesh" (Eph. 5:31; see also Gen. 2:24). Reflecting on a theology of marriage, Francis C. Rossow writes, "How somebody can be more than one person and yet only one essence is not only a mystery in the heavens but also a mystery right here on earth: whenever a man and a woman marry." He continues, "Upon the completion of a wedding ceremony, two separate, distinct persons somehow constitute only one essence—even though they remain two separate, distinct persons."[33]

Like other special-occasion sermons, the wedding sermon also has an evangelistic element to it. The preacher wants to demonstrate to the couple and the listeners the virtues of Christian marriage and that only those who have a foundation in Jesus Christ have the spiritual resources to make a marriage work. We want in our wedding preaching, as Paul urges Titus, to "make the teaching about God our Savior attractive" (Titus 2:10).

Although evangelism is a part of the wedding sermon, it is not the focus. Instead, our task is to direct the couple to their commitment to God and each other. We can explore practical elements of everyday marital behavior, commitment, and other features of the Christian life and emphasize that the couple's only hope is found in God in Christ and the mystery of being one in him. Through the preacher's instructions, others (the congregation) "overhear" what it means to follow Christ as a married couple.

William Skudlarek says that the purpose of preaching a wedding sermon is that "the gospel is preached to enable husband and wife to give themselves fully to each other in love and to call them and the witnessing congregation to celebrate that love as a sign of God's continuing presence in the church."[34]

What about leaving out the sermon? Is no sermon the best "sermon" to preach at a wedding?[35] Certainly in any Christian ceremony the Scriptures read and the prayers prayed serve to instruct the couple and the congregation in the Christian view of marriage. At best the couple and congregation hear the Word read. However, a clear, biblically based wedding sermon will bring focus to the ceremony. It is the time in the service to focus on God's Word. J. J. Van Oosterzee of a century ago says that as the pastor prepares and delivers the wedding sermon, "he must not therefore content himself with the reading of the ecclesiastical formulary, but, here too, give expression of the words of sacred discourse, in freely flowing the thoughts of a text of Holy Scripture."[36]

The strongest argument for including a sermon in a wedding service is that the wedding ceremony is an act of worship. Some have actually varied the pattern of the typical wedding service by holding the ceremony in the context of a regular worship service on Sunday morning.[37] Where there is worship, the Word of God is preached.

Saying It Right in the Sermon

Because the marriage ceremony is a worship service, the sermon should be God centered, rooted in biblical exegesis and theology, and audience related. Francis C. Rossow sums it up:

> Needless to say, the wedding sermon, like any other type of Christian sermon, should have something to say, should contain something of substance—without, of course, degenerating into an academic treatise. The wedding sermon should treat doctrine as well as dispense advice. It should be theological as well as "practical." It should deal with the mystery of marriage, and not only deal with the stuff of everyday living.[38]

Ministers want to have the following goals for their wedding sermons: Sermons should be focused, unique, brief, and clear. In order to accomplish these goals we first want to understand our listeners.

Linking with the Listeners

Ministers want wedding sermons that are connected to the Bible, but they also must be audience related. Preachers can get lost in preparing the sermon and forget that it is directed to people. They must get to know the couple. Many people assume that ministers intentionally become acquainted with the bride and groom. But pastors are busy and each wedding that comes along may seem as if it is just another appointment on the calendar. Getting to know the couple will help you know what to say in their wedding sermon. Invite them to a meal, host them in your home, create a comfortable atmosphere in the premarital sessions.[39] Ask them questions concerning their faith, relationship to the church,[40] family, friends, marital status, and children. Ask about the people invited to the wedding. Who are they? Why are they invited? Some attending the service may not be Christians. Some may have had a connection with the church at one time or another. Others have heard the words of the wedding service but they seemed empty to them. Some may be encouraged in their faith by the ceremony and the sermon.

Colorado pastor Ken Williams says that when he and his wife-to-be were searching for a minister to perform their wedding, they were turned off by the first pastor they went to see. He seemed busy, distracted, indifferent, and unfriendly. Williams remarks, "Many unchurched couples [and even churched] approach a minister's office with deep apprehension."[41] Be friendly toward any couple who comes to you. Being cordial is not merely part of a role preachers fill, but it is who we are to be.

The friendliness of the pastor and the investment of time and interest in the couple will be revealed when he or she stands up to preach. A congregation can tell whether the preacher cares about the couple and about the congregation. Sometimes ministers march through the liturgy with a voice that sounds distant, a kind of homiletical sing song. The sermon sounds canned. The preacher has not connected with the couple or the congregation. In contrast, genuine interest is apparent, as is genuine love.

An effective wedding sermon links with the listeners. Knowing the listeners will help the preacher shape a sermon that is biblically based, God centered, and listener related.

A Wedding Sermon Is Focused

Like any sermon, a wedding sermon should be focused. It must have purpose, the target the preacher wants to hit by preaching the sermon. The minister considers the kind of wedding (formal or informal), the setting (at the church building or out-of-doors), the couple (Christian, non-Christian, young, middle-aged, older, divorced, or widowed), and the congregation and develops the focus, the purpose, of the sermon. The preacher wants to be aware of the needs, questions, concerns, and resistance of the listener. Effective wedding sermons keep in mind the couple and the congregation. Both will help shape the focus of the sermon.

A good sermon has a written purpose statement. The purpose statement begins with the completion of the following sentence: As a result of hearing this sermon, my listeners will . . . For example:

> As a result of hearing this sermon, my listeners [the couple, and the congregation as they overhear] should know that Christ is the protector and pinnacle of their marriage.

> As a result of hearing this sermon, my listeners [the couple and congregation] will discover the thrill of a Christ-centered marriage.

> As a result of hearing this sermon, my listeners [the couple and congregation] will have confidence in the love of Christ as they love each other.[42]

A sermon with focus prevents the preacher from traveling all over the homiletical landscape. Knowing the purpose helps the preacher get to where he or she wants to go. The time for preaching at an occasion like this is usually limited, and preachers have a target to hit.

A Wedding Sermon Is Unique

There is no set way to develop a wedding sermon. The main thing to keep in mind is to communicate a central idea. Although the central idea is developed from the text, in a wedding sermon the couple and the congregation play a significant role in shaping the idea.

Some preachers have a standard wedding sermon. It may have a central idea, but it does not keep in mind the uniqueness of *this* wedding, *this* couple, or *this* congregation. Ministers may make the wedding sermon unique by shaping the central idea out of the following:

the theology of marriage
a great wedding text
a text as it bisects an aspect of the service
a text that intersects with the couple's interests or qualities
a text that reflects the personality of the couple
texts that capture the uniqueness of the couple as revealed
by the meanings of their names

A Christian couple may select a Bible passage that is meaningful to them. It may be a Scripture that has become important in their relationship, or the life verses of the bride and groom. However, most of the time the text selection and sermon content are left up to the minister. Certainly textual context is a guiding factor when preaching the sermon. A preacher can select an appropriate text on which to preach only after he or she has become sufficiently acquainted with the couple to know what would be meaningful to them and the listeners.

One factor in making a wedding sermon unique is its placement in the service. There are no rules as to when to preach the sermon but creative placement of the sermon will make the ceremony special. When Haddon Robinson officiated at his daughter's wedding, a number of non-Christians were expected to attend. Before the processional he gave an introductory homily. He explained to the congregation in a winsome way the reasons for the day and what would be taking place. The out-of-the-ordinary homily was an evangelistic opportunity and a teaching moment.

The emotions swirling around the wedding event differ from other special occasions. One preacher of wedding sermons remarks, "The effective message will tap into the emotions of the moment and communicate the truths of eternity. It will be both biblical and personal."[43] The key here is to take the universal truth found in the Scriptures and make it applicable to the couple who stand before you.

A Wedding Sermon Is Brief

Wordiness is not a virtue for wedding sermons. The sermon is only one part of the ceremony. Usually the couple and attendants stand throughout the service. The wedding comes at the end of a lot of preparation. Nerves are tense; people are tired. We want them to be drawn to what we have to say. We want them to want to hear the sermon. We must be brief.

Preachers who have focus and clarity will be able to be brief. A short, clear, central-idea wedding sermon will speak more loudly than a longer, meandering message. "Keep the message brief and to the point," warns Warren Wiersbe. He advises, "The most important thing about the wedding sermon is that it not sound like a sermon."[44]

What is a good length for a wedding sermon? I suggest five and at the most eight minutes. Remember, the preacher is not the center of the ceremony, nor is the couple—God is.

A Wedding Sermon Has a Clear Central Idea

One of my favorite wedding sermon approaches is to incorporate the names of the couple. At one ceremony

Patrick and Marcy were the couple standing before me. They were both Christians and chose Romans 12:9–13 as their wedding sermon passage. It reads:

> Let love be genuine; hate what is evil, hold fast to what is good; love one another with mutual affection; outdo one another in showing honor. Do not lag in zeal, be ardent in spirit, serve the Lord. Rejoice in hope, be patient in suffering, persevere in prayer. Contribute to the needs of the saints; extend hospitality to strangers.
>
> Romans 12:9–13 NRSV

First, I worked with the passage to discover the idea. My subject question was, What does Paul say Christian love looks like? The complement was, Love is motivated by the Lord who helps us to do good every day. The idea was, Paul says that love is motivated by the Lord who helps us to do good every day.

Next, I looked up the names of the couple. I keep a baby name book on hand. I discovered that Marcy means "from Mars" and Patrick means "noble, gentle." Keeping in mind the idea from the text, I worked with the names. The love Paul is talking about could not be expressed by his Roman readers on their own. It is a love that only comes from Christ, from out of this world (Mars/Marcy), and is gentle (gentle/Patrick) in everyday relationships. This is the challenge from the text for Christians to live in all of life and its relationships, even marriage.

The homiletical idea I shaped was, Christ is calling you to an out-of-this-world love that is gentle in all you do. In the homily I pointed out that it takes extraordinary love to be a Christian. The passage was written to instruct Christians how to love each other when it was not easy to do so. I applied the text to the couple's relationship as a married couple.

Multiple texts can be combined into one homiletical idea. Bill and Tara chose Colossians 1:15–20 and Matthew 25:31–46. Colossians features the image of the supremacy of Christ while Matthew images the Chief Shepherd at judgment. Tara means "rocky pinnacle" and William means "protector." After working on the complementary features of the passages, I created the homiletical idea, Christ is the protector and pinnacle of your marriage.

This process of developing a unique, tailored wedding sermon can be applied to the other suggestions for message topics listed above: theology, great text, service, interests, and personality of the couple. Both the message of the text and the uniqueness of the couple can be respected. God's Word will be heard by the couple and those who overhear. Both sets of listeners will be encouraged by a clear idea.

Preaching the Sermon

What are some things you want to keep in mind as you prepare to preach? Use concrete words. Use the images in the text that paint pictures in the minds of the listeners. Develop a clear outline. Work on flow. Work on transitions. Since the sermon is brief it will probably have only one or two segments that move up to or out of the idea. Write a manuscript. Once the outline and sermon are written, you will understand how the sermon moves and how it develops the homiletical idea. Test the length of your sermon by reading the manuscript out loud.

Ministers must remember that although they are familiar with the homiletical idea, their listeners are not. Repeating the idea at least three times, even in a brief sermon, will drive it home.

Now the day has arrived. The ceremony moves to the sermon. The couple holds hands as they face you. The bridal party looks on. The congregation has their eyes on you. You begin to speak. You have developed a sermon that is biblical and listener sensitive. Some things you want to keep in mind as you speak are these:

Be joyful
Get and maintain eye contact with the couple
    and congregation
Be personal, warm, and friendly
Be conversational
Articulate, and project your voice
Know the names of the bride and groom
Preach without notes
Be brief

The wedding is a special day in the life of the couple. You can help make it special. Communicate the joy of the day with your attitude and actions. Your presence can set the tone for the service, which is joy and celebration!

Eye contact allows you to connect with your listeners. By cultivating eye contact, the preacher is able to demonstrate warmth and friendliness. Lively eye contact, smiles, appropriate gestures, and tone of voice will draw in one's listeners. A conversational tone will also aid in communication.[45]

Speak clearly (articulate), and project your voice. You are speaking to the couple *and* to the congregation. Everybody needs to hear. Technology may not be available or functioning so the pastor must adapt. I have performed weddings in homes, backyards, and forests. One friend conducted a ceremony from a hot air balloon! Needless to say he had to project!

Your best communication comes when you preach without notes. Not only will you exercise good eye contact and a personal and conversational style, but also brevity. Preaching without notes does not mean extemporaneous preaching. It provides discipline and means that you have worked on what you will say and gone over it many times. When you speak you sound extemporaneous.

Practicing to Preach

1. Select one of the six sources of wedding sermon topics: the theology of marriage, a great wedding text, a text as it bisects an aspect of the service, a text that intersects with the couple's interests or qualities, a text that reflects the personality of the couple, texts that capture the uniqueness of the couple as revealed by the meanings of their names.
2. Find the subject, complement, and idea for the text.
3. List the images and repeated words or phrases found in the text.
4. List the characteristics of the couple and the congregation. How should the ceremony be affected by these characteristics?
5. Write a purpose statement: As a result of hearing this wedding sermon, my listeners [couple and congregation] will . . .
6. Write a homiletical idea.
7. Write a sermon outline.
8. Write a sermon manuscript.

Shelf-Wise

Hedahl, Susan K. *Preaching the Wedding Sermon.* St. Louis: Chalice Press, 1999.

Martos, Joseph. *Doors to the Sacred: A Historical Introduction to the Sacraments in the Christian Church.* London: SCM Press, 1981.

Schlafer, David J. *What Makes This Day Different? Preaching Grace on Special Occasions.* Boston: Cowley, 1998.

Wiersbe, Warren W. *The Dynamics of Preaching.* Grand Rapids: Baker, 1999.

3

Funeral Sermons

No pastoral responsibility is more demanding than ministering comfort to people who are shocked and bereaved because of the death of a loved one.

Warren W. Wiersbe

Before I preached a Sunday morning sermon at my first church, I had preached my first funeral sermon. On Tuesday I moved into the parsonage and on Friday I had the funeral. Bess Thomas was 102 and, I think, was waiting for the new minister of the First Baptist Church to arrive and then she would die.

I hardly knew where to begin. During my seminary summer internship, I had assisted with a few funerals and even conducted one myself, but this time I was on my own. Faced with the challenge of preaching at Bess Thomas's funeral, her long years and rich faith abounding, I met with the family, combed the Scriptures, thumbed through resources, and wrote my sermon. Still, I wished I was better prepared.

Although there is more written about the funeral than any other special occasion, it is a service for which most pastors are least ready. Death is not planned. Funerals intrude on your appointment book. The funeral message is yet one more sermon to preach during the week. It can be a chore but it can also be a wonderful opportunity for ministry.

The History of the Funeral Sermon

Funeral speeches have a long history. Since biblical days Jewish funerals have included eulogies. David's eulogy over Saul and Jonathan is perhaps the most famous (2 Sam. 1:19–27). During the rabbinic period the eulogy was an established practice.[1] Eulogies were based on Scripture and embellished with parables. The object was to arouse loud laments and weeping.[2] But speakers were warned not to overstate the qualities of the deceased: "Just as the dead are punished [for their sins], so funeral orators are punished [for exaggerating the merits of the dead]."[3]

Funeral eulogies for a person of outstanding piety or scholarship took place at the synagogue, but common people were carried to the cemetery, where the service was held.[4] In the sixteenth century, eulogies for a deceased scholar might be given each day during the week beginning with the burial. One rabbi noted that he preached funeral sermons on the death of a scholar the day of the burial, the seventh day, the thirteenth day, and at the end of the year.[5]

The Greek eulogy had many hundreds of years of tradition behind it, coming from the literary genre known as the encomium, which was one type of funeral observance. The other was the treatise on grief or consolation, which was often given in the form of a letter. The Greek funeral speech grew out of the commemoration of soldiers who had died in battle for their country.[6]

Isocrates (427–329 B.C.), the great publicist and teacher of rhetoric, was probably the first to compose a funeral oration on an individual. The funeral speech was perfected by rhetoricians, those who studied speech. Menander (342–290 B.C.), the Greek rhetorician, divides the encomium into two classes—for the living and for the dead. The latter, the "epitaph," is further divided into four types: (1) The pure encomium, which speaks of one long dead and is primarily concerned with praise; (2) the epitaph, which has two forms, the first or general type and the second or particular type, deals with an individual who has recently died and usually combines praise with consolation and lament; (3) the monody, a brief but intense lament; and (4) the consolatory speech, which is similar to the monody but has much more emphasis on consolation.[7]

The practice of the epitaph was cultivated in the Greek schools of rhetoric and was skillfully practiced by such famous sophists as Libanius, Himerius, and Themistius in the second half of the fourth century A.D. It is not surprising to discover the powerful influence that Greek rhetoric had on Christian funeral preaching. Himerius of Athens is likely to have been one of the chief teachers of Gregory Nazianzen, the great Christian preacher.[8] Nazianzen was the first to initiate the adaptation of the Greek funeral oration to Christian use.[9]

Although similar to the Greek encomium, the Christian funeral provided consolation rooted in the doctrines of the Christian faith. Most often the focus was the resurrection of Jesus Christ from the dead. Greek rhetoric certainly influenced the early church fathers. Historian Martin R. P. McGuire reflects:

> They could not escape the literary interests and tastes of their environment. It was only natural, under the circum-

stances, that they should be zealous to use their literary training and talents in the service of their faith, and that in so doing they should adapt long-established pagan literary genres to their use.[10]

While Gregory Nazianzen and Gregory of Nyssa reworked the pagan Greek rhetorical form for Christian use, they likely influenced Ambrose as he introduced the Christian funeral oration into Latin literature.[11]

Preaching was part of funeral worship in the early church. When the Edict of Toleration (A.D. 325) was issued, a liturgy in a public worship building either preceded or followed the procession to the grave. This liturgy used forms similar to those of the Sunday celebration with prayers, Scripture readings, preaching, and finally the Eucharist.[12]

During the next ten centuries Roman Catholic traditions dominated. The use of liturgy and ritual characterized Christian worship. The funeral became increasingly ritualized with less emphasis on the funeral sermon.

Reformers like Martin Luther (1483–1546) also stressed the funeral sermon. The point of the funeral shifted from assisting the deceased in their passage to heaven and became instead an object lesson for the living.[13] Lutherans often had a homily at the home of the deceased, at the church building, or at the graveside.[14]

European Reformed churches held that funerals were essentially not the responsibility of the church. However, Pullain, the minister of the Church of the Strangers in Glastonbury at the time of King Edward VI and also of the French congregation meeting in the town of Frankfort, used prayers, readings, and a short sermon at the graveside. It is doubtful that Calvin did so.[15]

The funeral sermons of Puritan New England reflected the treatise on grief or consolation from Greek rhetoric. The sermons were preached but then were printed and distributed. Harry Stout comments:

To commemorate the faith of New England's first native-born generation, ministers began printing funeral sermons, which had as their overriding theme the enduring piety of the deceased. In the 1690s, examples of this genre of sermon constituted the most numerous printed sermons in New England. Like the printed final sermons of the founders, funeral sermons used death to underscore the passage of generations and the covenant's continuity. Above all, they urged the rising generation to remember their predecessors and imitate their piety. Most of the subjects of funeral sermons were second-generation ministers or their wives, but prominent lay leaders were also remembered.[16]

First-generation seventeenth-century American Puritans did not allow funeral sermons on the day of the burial. However, it soon became customary to give them on the Sunday after the funeral. Later in the century the sermon was given on the evening of the funeral. John Cotton (1584–1652) preached the first known funeral sermon in 1646 on the Sunday following a burial. James Fitch preached the first published funeral sermon in New England in 1672.[17] Later, second-generation Puritan Cotton Mather (1663–1728) encouraged the use of prayers and "a short *Speech* at the *Grave*."[18] In Britain Puritans were divided over the issue. The Westminster Assembly (1643–1649) discussed the suitability of funeral sermons for six days. The English approved of them; the Scottish delegates denounced them.[19]

A funeral sermon that John Donne (1572–1631) preached in 1626 demonstrates the lengthiness of some funeral sermons.[20] It is also typical of the published sermons of public figures in both Britain and the United States.

Methodists in Britain also preached at funerals: "And in burying the dead, the officiating preacher frequently delivers a short appropriate discourse to those who are present."[21] Eighteenth-century American Puritan funerals became elaborate as did funerals in Britain. In 1771 London Baptists mourned the death of Dr. John Gill. A somber procession took the mourners to the church building, where the funeral preacher addressed the crowd from a pulpit hung with black cloth.[22]

In the nineteenth century, funeral sermons became more common among various denominations.[23] Sermons were often published as booklets or part of larger sermon collections. They lamented the death of prominent civic leaders, pastors, youths, and teachers.[24] Sermon length typically was forty-five minutes to an hour or more.

Ozora Davis observed that at one point during the early twentieth century the funeral sermon was largely abandoned in some circles. He seemed to think that it was a "great relief to the preacher and certainly in the interests of good taste and truthfulness" not to have a sermon but rely on the liturgy. There were some occasions, however, when a brief sermon was given.[25]

Today funeral observances vary. There is the decided trend toward graveside services. Some elect to have their loved one buried with a memorial service and sermon scheduled weeks or even months later. Most Christian services have a scripturally based funeral sermon as part of the liturgy, while others eulogize the deceased by readings, poems, memorabilia, and reminiscences. After studying modern funeral practices, Thomas G. Long observes that the role of the funeral is changing:

> American funeral services are assuming an upbeat, almost festive, mood, and death rituals often are taking on a "monogrammed" look with intimate artifacts of the deceased in evidence everywhere. The funeral home will often display photographs, trophies, writings, and art objects of the person who has died; more and more, personal items like jewelry, texts of favorite songs and poems, even tennis and golf balls are placed in the casket; and reflections and

reminiscences about the deceased are included in the funeral liturgy.[26]

Long concludes, "Since the cross makes so little sense, golf balls and charm bracelets move into the symbolic vacuum."[27]

Throughout the centuries words of comfort have been spoken at funerals. Today preachers face a great challenge as they preach Christ in a culture that does not know much about him and in a culture that avoids thinking about death. Christian preachers can capture the moment to help mourners gain encouragement and strength found in God.

Sermon versus Eulogy

The funeral sermon and the eulogy are different, even opposed to each other. Simply put, *eulogy* means "good words" and the eulogy focuses on the life of the person who has died. What is appropriate to say? The eulogy is especially problematic when preachers make saints out of sinners in their funeral sermons. Is there an appropriate place for the eulogy? It has been part of our common funeral tradition. Those who argue against it say that it takes the focus away from God and places emphasis on the person who has died. We must consider whether this is something to be avoided. Some preachers prefer to drop any reference to the person who has died. This is particularly the case in Catholic circles.[28]

The concern is that a eulogy "is mistaken for the gospel."[29] However, one has argued, "To speak about the person who has died does not necessarily mean that the person has become the focus of the homily."[30] If the entire emphasis of the sermon is on the person and the good things he or she has done or what a good person he or she was— or what the preacher or those who gather want this person to be—then the sermon would be out of focus with reality and Christian truth. It does not need to be this way.

The matter is one of focus. Certainly the message of the Bible must be in focus. Eulogizing the life of the individual in submission to the living Word will not necessarily put the sermon out of focus. With the sermon firmly locked on the text, one can talk about and even celebrate the life of the person who has died and not damage the unchanging truth of God. Besides, the death of this person is the reason why people have gathered.

The following are questions preachers can ask to keep their sermons in focus:

Does what I say about the person point people to Christ?

Am I ignoring the sinfulness of the person who has died?

What does the text say about the person who has died?

Does what I say stop with the person or move from there to Christ?

A possible solution to the concern about the eulogy is to give it at a time separate from the sermon. As the minister, you can invite others to speak. This feature gives mourners the opportunity to participate in the service and to express their grief.

Eulogy was woven into the fabric of funeral orations in ancient Judaism. Its threads span the centuries and are part of the cloth of today's funeral preaching. The fibers mesh with the truth of the gospel. In the funeral sermon the tapestry is displayed and God gets all the credit.

The Theology of Funeral Sermons

We need to have a theology of death. More particularly, preachers need to know why they preach at funerals.[31] Nineteenth-century Dutch theologian J. J. Van Oosterzee observed: "According to the Wurtemberg ecclesiastical ordinance, the funeral address is designed to answer a threefold end. It ought to be 'a public confession of the Christian hope of the resurrection, a last testimony of love, an earnest reminder of the approaching hour of death.'"[32]

Theologically, the funeral service is an offering of worship to God. Edgar N. Jackson says, "The funeral service is the opportunity for an act of worship that is neither trivial nor trite."[33] The hope of the gospel in Jesus Christ is to be the center of a funeral sermon. At a funeral, death is there, people are there, and God is there—and hope is there in Christ.[34] With the Scripture as the focus, the listeners are given comfort from the eternal truths of the Christian faith. As preachers, we want to be clear in our preaching about Christ and the wonder of his love and the abundance of his grace.

Thomas G. Long comments, "What a Christian funeral does primarily is to provide a suitable structure and language for the worship of God at the time of death."[35] Mark Chapman agrees, "[The] authentic Christian language at a funeral is that which says that God the Father has raised from the dead his crucified Son, Jesus Christ, and in that has given his Holy Spirit that we might receive his Spirit of life and so share in the triumph of life over death that Jesus Christ has won."[36]

Ministers debate the role of evangelism in funeral preaching.[37] The discussion has more to do with the degree or extent of evangelism than whether to evangelize. Preaching by its very nature is evangelistic. Some see funerals as an exclusive opportunity to evangelize aggressively. Tony Walter writes about a friend who left the church in which he had been raised. When his father died, the pastor conducted a three-hour funeral. The sermon "was directed mainly at reminding the son of the joys of dying with and the terrors of dying without Christ, calling him to repent and return to the fold."[38] Walter's story may be extreme, but our goal in funeral preaching is to point listeners to the promise of the gospel.

Some may suggest that the family is too upset to be able to hear a sermon. "Just pray and read a few Scriptures," they say. Some service books provide the possibility of a sermon but do not require it.[39] But preaching at funerals provides occasions for the Word to encourage believers and to take root in the lives of those who rarely hear or may never have heard the gospel.

Nineteenth-century theologian Christlieb reflected on preaching at a funeral: "The Funeral Address belongs to the most difficult, but also to the most beautiful and effective functions of the pastor. Its task is not to drive away the God-sent sorrow, but to purify and hallow it."[40] When we preach the Word of God, the witnessing community is able to agree with it and are given encouragement to live by it. Our faith is not people centered but God centered and is rooted in the Scripture.

Saying It Right in the Sermon

As we have covered in the chapter so far, we want the funeral sermon to be Bible based, Christ centered, gospel oriented, and comfort producing. These elements will help the preacher communicate to his or her listeners a solid, empathetic sermon. Additionally, all preaching must be listener oriented.

Linking with the Listeners

Funeral sermons that are most effective are connected to the Bible and to the listeners and fit into the flow of the worship service. The preacher wants to understand the deceased and the family and to appreciate the listeners who will be attending the funeral. Preaching for a family in the church is one thing, but shaping a sermon for someone who is not from your church is another. As in most special-occasion preaching, if you get to know the family of the deceased, you will have an understanding of who the listeners will be at the funeral service.

Alvin Rueter reflects on how he struggled with connecting with his listeners—and failed:

> I remember a funeral for a man who found me hard to appreciate. First we had a service in our church. Then we had another one forty miles away, where he had grown up and where he would be buried. This allowed acquaintances in each neighborhood to attend, but since the family and some of the friends would be at both places, I felt I should prepare two funerals. It didn't help that it was a hot and dusty day. I'm afraid my exasperation showed. A few days later, the man's daughter came to see me. She was bitter: "No feelings. So impersonal." She was right.[41]

If we want to make our funerals effective, then they must be personal.[42] How can pastors make their funeral sermons personal? The answer to this question depends on a number of factors, including the length of the pastor's tenure at the church and the relationship with the family. One of the keys to personalizing funerals is keeping up-to-date records of pastoral visits.[43] Records of family members' names, relationships, hobbies, interests, and talents can be information woven into the sermon.

When contacted about the death, visit the family. Take notes. Ask questions or make leading statements such as these: "Tell me about your memories of her." "What do you want people to remember about him?" "What was his favorite hymn and Bible passage?" When visiting the home, be aware of photographs and other evidences of hobbies or interests that the person who died may have had: "What were her hobbies or interests?" "What things come to mind when you think of her?" Questions like these will guide the shaping of the funeral sermon.

Good preachers know the power of relating to the listener. The experiences I had in the pastorate, as I walked with families through grief, forged a connection that lasted long after the funeral sermon and service. It is called ministry. We can form the links with our listeners by caring for them, by being with them, by loving them, by knowing them, and by pointing them to the Scriptures. As preachers we have the privilege of coming alongside a family during a difficult time. We can make a difference in their relationship with Christ, perhaps more than we realize. One pastor I know says, "I don't do funerals. I take care of families during funerals."

A Funeral Sermon Is Focused

Funeral sermons must be focused. The purpose of a funeral sermon differs from other types of preaching because of the occasion. Andrew Blackwood advised that the purpose of the funeral sermon "is pastoral rather than evangelistic. The aim is to comfort the friends who mourn, that is, to strengthen their hearts in God."[44] "Remember, your *primary* task is to comfort, not to evangelize," remarks Bryan Chapell. "Even though evangelisic truths are presented, this is a funeral sermon. The *main* purpose is to bring the hope of the gospel to loved ones facing the pain of death."[45]

Ministers are to point men and women to Jesus Christ in the funeral sermon. Warren Wiersbe agrees: "It's my conviction that the purpose of the funeral message is to exalt Jesus Christ as the adequate answer to every problem."[46]

Biblically based sermons are to be audience oriented. A funeral sermon is not addressed to the deceased. It is spoken to the mourners—the family and friends. Ministers are to shape purpose statements that keep in mind the Bible, the listeners, and the occasion for people to hear about the hope found in Jesus Christ. The following are sample purpose statements:

As a result of hearing this sermon, my listeners [mourners] will be comforted by God's presence in their lives.

As a result of hearing this sermon, my listeners [mourners] will be grateful to God for salvation in Jesus Christ.

As a result of hearing this sermon, my listeners [mourners] will know that at the end of time we will not mourn but will praise God.

A Funeral Sermon Is Unique

Some preachers use a "cookie-cutter sermon" for every funeral they preach. It is tempting to do, but try to avoid it.[47] Every funeral is unique. Every person who has died is unique. That is why the standard, repeated, retreaded sermon will not do.

A friend of mine told me a true story about a woman in Michigan whose husband had died. The funeral director asked her, "How much do you want to give the minister as an honorarium—$25 or $150?" She told him that she would like to wait until after the service before she decided.

The preacher gave his canned funeral sermon, same text, same prayers. She had heard him deliver the same sermon several times before. On the way out of the funeral home, the widow said to the funeral director, "$25."

Perhaps a funeral director asks you to preach a sermon for someone you don't know. You get the call the day before the funeral. What do you do? It's fair to use a text you've used before, but shape it for this particular funeral. Eltin Griffin urges, "What matters most in the special occasion homily is the particular twist that the preacher can give to it."[48]

The twist that makes funeral sermons unique can happen by shaping the central idea out of the following:

the theology of grace, salvation, forgiveness, faith

death as the Christian's hope

a great funeral text

a text that intersects with the interests of the deceased

a text that reflects the personality and character of the deceased

the favorite text of the deceased

a text that captures the uniqueness of the deceased by using his or her name or occupation

The family may suggest a text from any of the above categories. The decision may be left to the minister. Pastors should assess the faith of the deceased and the family before settling on a text. When this is done, a text can be selected and made specific to the occasion.

A Funeral Sermon Is Brief

Funeral sermons should be brief. Sermons in other days could last hours. A conservative guess places the funeral sermon of Ambrose and Gregory at seventy-five to ninety minutes.[49] Some nineteenth-century funeral preaching lasted at least as long.[50] Calvin Ratz says, "A funeral message isn't lengthy, but it should be long enough to provide substance for faith to grasp."[51]

If published sermons from today are any indication, funeral sermons are short. Unlike the ninety-minute sermon mentioned above, ministers generally agree on an upper limit of ten to fifteen minutes.[52]

A Funeral Sermon Has a Clear Central Idea

Once you have a background on the person who has died, the next step is to select a text. In his book on funeral preaching, Andrew Blackwood reflects on the selection of the biblical text: "It may not prove easy to select a passage that is sure to meet the needs of the approaching hour. . . . The text should be striking. It should arrest attention and fix itself at once in the memory."[53]

In preparation for funeral preaching, Calvin Ratz advises that he will "tend to stay away from the most obvious texts. But, [he] tries to stay away from obscure texts."[54] Warren Wiersbe agrees: "Don't build the message on obscure and unusual texts or on texts that will demand extended explanations."[55] On the other hand, an obscure text may be the most meaningful and memorable. Tailor your sermon to the occasion and the audience, but remember: A complicated text and exegesis will only frustrate and confuse the listeners. Wiersbe notes, "As people go through the valley, they can't handle the abstractions of systematic theology but they can see the biblical images that reveal a caring and comforting Savior."[56]

One of the most in-depth practical studies on the funeral sermon was done by Earl Daniels in the mid-1930s.[57] His study has a timelessness about it, and his suggestions for shaping the funeral sermon are worth noting. Daniels classifies funeral sermons into three catagories: biographical, occasional, and doctrinal:

> The Biographical Sermon arises out of the life experiences of the deceased. It is the presentation of the importance of that life to the community.

> The Occasional Sermon deals with unusual situations. The deceased may have died under unusual circumstances such as murder, suicide, or accident.

The Doctrinal Sermon centers its attention, not upon the individual, nor the special circumstances, but upon the experience of Death and the problems which it raises in our minds.[58]

Biographical Preaching

Daniels's classifications are helpful because they provide categories that might otherwise not be considered by the preacher. In biographical preaching the focus is not necessarily on the person, but effort is made to remain Christ focused with a personal perspective. Biblical truths are not obscured by reference to the life of the person. Instead, as Mark Coppenger observes about his own preaching, "Simply try to use an item from the deceased's life to introduce a truth from God, not build a case for the person's glory."[59]

A biographical sermon may incorporate a person's occupation, his or her role and contribution to the life of a local church, special interests, civic activities, friends, hobbies, or favorite things or personal characteristics.[60] The sermon may include humorous stories from the family, stories that the deceased used to tell about him or herself, humorous accounts from relatives, friends, or neighbors.[61] John Mansell suggests, "Search for a phrase that shows how the departed lived life." This phrase may express the merging of the text and the person's life, which becomes the homiletical idea.[62]

Jim Procious was a dear Christian man from my first church. He gave of himself and of his time. He was precious. The words sound alike, *Procious* and *precious*. In my sermon for his funeral, I played off these two words, leading the listeners to Psalm 116:15, "Precious in the sight of the Lord is the death of his saints."

Another way to approach biographical preaching is to do a "life review." Psalm 84 was the text a pastor friend of mine used for the funeral of seventy-three-year-old Gene Salter. For years Gene had served as the usher for the worship services. The sermon began with the hope that is found in Christ and that the deceased enjoyed that hope while living and enjoys it in eternity. The pastor then traced Gene's life in light of Christian hope and spoke of how he contributed to the life of the church. He was "proud to be a doorkeeper for Christ," said the pastor, who wove the biography of Gene into the sermon, all the while keeping the focus on God and his Word.[63]

Focusing on the name or occupation of the deceased is another angle for the biographical sermon. One of my students preached a funeral for a ninety-one-year-old man who was an expert in fingerprinting. The text was 2 Timothy 4:6–8:

> For I am already being poured out like a drink offering, and the time has come for my departure. I have fought the good fight, I have finished the race, I have kept the faith. Now there is in store for me the crown of righteousness, which the Lord, the righteous Judge, will award to me on that day—and not only to me, but also to all who have longed for his appearing.

He talked about the mark the apostle Paul left on all those with whom he came into contact. Then he spoke about the mark that John Growley left on the lives of others. He told about John's occupation of reading, collecting, and identifying fingerprints. The homiletical idea was, John left his mark on this world, and his was the mark of Christ.[64]

A homiletical twist on the biographical sermon is to turn the lens from the person who died onto the mourners who listen and are struggling to live. Long notes:

> In funerals, life stories of those who have died and the stories of those who must go on without them are also told, but this telling is done in the framework of the larger gospel narrative. The stories told at a funeral push beyond biography to baptismal narrative.[65]

59

The biographical sermon does not obscure the listener from seeing the ultimate focus, God.

Occasional Sermon

The occasional sermon fits the sermon to the circumstances surrounding the funeral. With alliterative flair, Daniels designates the first type of circumstance as "Capitalizing Coincidences" and the second as "Dealing with Difficult Situations."[66] As for the "Coincidences," the significance of the person's death may be magnified if he or she was young or old, married, single, with children, or childless. Or the funeral or death may take place on the anniversary of a personal event, birthday, anniversary, or holiday. Even weather conditions during the day of death or of the funeral or family relationships may be factors the preacher may use to direct men and women to the hope of the gospel.

The way the person died may also affect the sermon, particularly in cases of suicide, murder, devastating illness, or accident. Naming the cause of death will allow listeners to begin their recovery from grief at the same starting point.[67]

The death of infants, children, or young adults is especially difficult. I conducted a funeral for quadruplets who died before birth. The young Christian parents mourned the loss of their children. The text was Revelation 7:9–17. The exegetical idea for the passage is, Those who endure the struggle of living out their faith are protected by God, who will care for them forever. Keeping in mind the occasion, the couple, and the congregation, I developed the homiletical idea, At the end of the story our tears are gone and God is praised.

Another difficult situation that every pastor faces is conducting the funeral of a non-Christian. Preaching at the funeral of someone who has rejected Christ is tough, no matter how one looks at it. You want to be sensitive to the people related to and associated with the deceased. Through conversations with the family you will be able to judge their receptivity to the gospel and determine the best way to preach Christ.

Doctrinal Sermon

Daniels's final category is the doctrinal sermon, which selects a text that speaks of Christian hope. Preachers can talk about the greatness and the goodness of God and the Christian hope of future life in the presence of God.[68]

Bryan Wilkerson taught listeners about Christian hope from Romans 8:28–30 when he conducted the funeral for a young girl who died unexpectedly. His homiletical idea came from a movie that was popular at the time he preached—*A River Runs through It.* Wilkerson wove the text and the occasion together for his homiletical idea, There's a river that runs through it, and that river is called the purpose of God.[69]

Another way to shape the doctrinal sermon is to relate the funeral sermon to the church year and specific events in the life of Christ. Here the theological focus is provided by a text appropriate to the season in the liturgical year, and the person's life is tied in to it. A funeral during Advent might suggest texts of preparation, hope, or expectation.[70]

Memorial Sermon

Memorial services are becoming more common. They may be conducted days, weeks, or even months after a death. For any number of reasons, family members or friends may not be able to gather immediately after a death to mourn, so they hold a memorial service for the deceased at a later date. One July day I conducted a memorial service for Ruth Reno, who had died the previous December. The annual family reunion was slated for July, and that's when the family scheduled the memorial service. In the sermon that celebrated her life, I wove Psalm 103:13–19 together with excerpts from letters I had received from this dear saint. The homiletical idea was, God loves us—he knows we need him—and we know we need him too.

Cremation may also be a reason why people choose to have a memorial service. My father requested that he be cremated when he died. Since our town didn't have a crematorium we weren't able to have his remains present at the funeral, so we chose to have a memorial service.

Sermons at memorial services mirror those at funerals. The only difference is the absence of the body and the time between the death and the service.

Preaching the Sermon

The funeral sermon is about to begin. You have met with the family, grasped the composition of the audience, wrestled with the text, and written the sermon. Ministers want to keep some things in mind as they preach:

Get and maintain eye contact with the mourners and
   congregation
Be warm, compassionate, and friendly
Watch body language and tone of voice
Repeat the homiletical idea at least three times
Be conversational
Articulate, and project your voice
Know the name of the deceased and the family
Be empathetic
Preach without notes
Be brief

Some of these points are the same as for other special-occasion preaching. For funeral preaching perhaps some of the above need further emphasis. The way you preach communicates more than what you have to say. One preacher put it this way: "The worst of all failures at a funeral is to be formal, professional, and cold."[71] Another minister wrote, "The manner and method of the minister, as well as his message, determine the mood of the memorial service. These intangibles are hard to reproduce in print."[72]

British preacher Wesley Carr notes, "Because of the emotional dislocation experienced by the bereaved, they can rarely hear what is actually said. Odd remarks may stick, but people remember demeanour and attitude more than content."[73]

Preachers should come across as warm, personal, and confident. Robert Blair claims, "The confidence you demonstrate and the message you bring will not only help the mourners, it can also lead to your own spiritual well-being and renewal. I say this because death not only takes families by surprise, it also takes the clergy by surprise."[74] Stuart Briscoe agrees: "We should be as warm and personal as we are able; firm in our articulation of biblical truth; and as natural, conversational, and empathetic as possible, to avoid sounding sermonic."[75]

These are good reminders for any preacher who wants to preach a central idea but does not want to get in its way. Sometimes we have a good, clear idea but we obscure it by what we say, how we say it, or what we do.

Practicing to Preach _____

1. Select one of the three categories for funeral sermons: the biographical sermon (using a text that intersects with the interests of the deceased, the favorite text of the deceased, a text that reflects the personality and character of the deceased, a text that captures the

uniqueness of the deceased by using his or her name or occupation); the occasional sermon (a great funeral text); the doctrinal sermon (death as the Christian's hope, the theology of grace, salvation, forgiveness, faith).

2. Find the subject, complement, and idea for the text.
3. List the images and repeated words or phrases found in the text.
4. List the characteristics of the deceased and mourners. How should the ceremony be affected by these characteristics?
5. Write a purpose statement: As a result of hearing this funeral sermon, my listeners [mourners] will . . .
6. Write a homiletical idea.
7. Write a sermon outline.
8. Write a sermon manuscript.

Shelf-Wise

Blackwood, Andrew W. *The Funeral: A Source Book for Ministers.* Philadelphia: Westminster, 1942.

Lloyd, Dan S. *Leading Today's Funerals.* Grand Rapids: Baker, 1997.

Long, Thomas G. "The Funeral: Changing Patterns and Teachable Moments." *Journal for Preachers* 19, no. 3 (Easter 1996): 3–8.

Mansell, John S. *The Funeral.* Nashville: Abingdon, 1998.

Schmitz, Barbara G. *The Life of Christ and the Death of a Loved One: Crafting the Funeral Homily.* Lima, Ohio: CSS Publishing, 1995.

4

Baptism and Infant Presentation Sermons

A responsible biblical and theological approach for ministers is to intentionally link together the sermon and ceremony.

Baptism (infant or believers') or infant presentation/parental dedication declares the wonder of God's grace in Jesus Christ. Occasions like these are dramatic acts of faith and demonstrate the Christian's dependence on God. Preaching at these occasions focuses on the significance of growth in discipleship and obedience to Christ.

I was baptized in a cow pond on the Dale and Frances Currie farm in New Castle, Pennsylvania, in August 1972. The sun warmed the earth. A summer breeze blew. Three candidates for baptism stepped into the cool waters and I was one of them. The pastor gave a brief sermon from Romans 6. Following the sermon, I was asked a series of questions, to which I responded by verbally confessing my faith in the Lord Jesus Christ. I was then plunged beneath the water and baptized in the name of the Father, the Son, and the Holy Spirit. As I look back on my baptism, I realize that what rounded it out was the clear word from the Bible by Pastor Paul R. LeVan. He preached. Then he baptized.

Years later I was the pastor. Standing before me in a church worship service on a Sunday morning were Bob and Sherry, cradling Bobby in their arms, presenting him to the Lord and dedicating themselves to God to love and care for their son. They were proud parents, hopeful of Christ's care for Bobby and for themselves as parents. Bobby was precious and full of promise. I asked the mother and father questions about their dedication to raising their child in the faith and asked the congregation if they would covenant with the Lord to nurture and love Bobby in Christ. I prayed for Bob and Sherry and Bobby, holding him in my arms. Then I preached a sermon.

After time in pastoral ministry, I returned to formal study at Princeton Theological Seminary. One of my classes focused on pastoral ministry and special occasions. Since I was a Baptist at a Presbyterian seminary, the baptism section of the course presented me with some unfamiliar concepts. I learned how to perform infant baptisms. As in a believer's baptism service or at a service for the presentation of infants/dedication of parents, a sermon is expected.

I learned a lot from my Presbyterian friends. Most of all I learned that despite the differences in the when and the how of baptism, the ceremony has an important place in the life of the church. I am convinced that baptism or infant presentation should not be separated from the sermon.

The History of the Baptism and Infant Presentation Sermon

When we thumb through the New Testament to discover the place of preaching and baptism, our attention is directed to the Acts of the Apostles. Most of the sermons recorded in Acts may be called "missionary preaching." There is no formal worship service in which these sermons were preached. Hughes Oliphant Old comments on the relation of preaching to worship and baptism:

> The point we want to make is that the missionary sermon, no matter where it is preached, no matter how secular its literary form, whether it be a philosophical polemic in Athens or a defense in a court of law—the missionary sermon always implies a call to repentance and baptism. Missionary preaching is part of the sacrament of baptism. The missionary sermon belongs to the substance of a true celebration of baptism, as to the penitential sermon and the catechetical sermon. . . . When Jesus commissioned his apostles to make disciples of all nations by baptizing them and teaching them to observe all things which he had commanded them, it was exactly this that Jesus had in mind.[1]

What we find in the first through the third centuries is that Christian worship developed more formal patterns. The celebration of baptism included prayer and the reading and preaching of the Scripture, which seems to indicate that the reading and preaching of the Scripture had a prominent place in the worship of Christian churches.[2]

Throughout the latter part of the third century and into the fourth and fifth centuries, the church developed the practice of instruction of believers prior to the actual ceremony of baptism. This was called catechetical preaching. Catechumens were unbaptized people who had been accepted by the church for instruction in hope that baptism would follow. Catechumens were admitted to the first part of the worship service, then dismissed before the offerings.[3] Toward the end of the fourth century catechetical preaching grew in importance. Some of its aspects were evangelism, a recounting of salvation history, and moral teaching. Moral catechizing had begun to develop years earlier, as evidenced in texts like 1 Peter 3–5, 1 Timothy, and Ephesians 5. Doctrine also was taught in catechetical preaching. The baptismal rites of Milan at the end of the fourth century indicate that a time was set aside for teaching the candidates the creed.[4]

Tertullian, Ambrose, Cyril of Jerusalem, and John Chrysostom among others preached various types of catechetical sermons. Ambrose's kind of preaching focused on training new Christians, converted from the Hellenistic mystery religions.[5] John Chrysostom preached an introductory sermon at the beginning of thirty days of catechetical instruction. At the end he preached a sermon explaining the rites and ceremony associated with baptism. After the catechumens were baptized on Easter morning, he preached to them on the importance of what they had experienced. His main purpose in the sermon was to tell the catechumens that in the sacrament of baptism they had obligated themselves to live the kind of life Jesus had taught. Finally, during Easter week, Chrysostom addressed the newly baptized every day on various aspects of the Christian life.[6]

For Augustine, baptism was just as closely connected to the Word as was the celebration of the Supper. His catechetical sermons on 1 John demonstrate how baptism required Christian discipleship. The act of baptism not only seals the promises proclaimed in the gospel, but it also demands a systematic, lifelong study of God's Word. As Hughes Oliphant Old observes about Augustine's catechetical preaching, "The whole preaching ministry of the Church is found in the sign of baptism."[7]

By the time of Leo the Great (ca. 400–461), the baptism of adults in Rome became less frequent and the baptism of infants became more common.[8] However, apart from this development, there is no evidence of a ceremony to dedicate infants during this time. Some historians suggest that the Paulicians, a religious group living around the 6th–12th century, had some form of dedication service because they refused to have their infants baptized.[9]

What develops at the time of the Reformation is the baptismal exhortation, a short sermon on the meaning of baptism. The Reformers in Strasbourg shaped the baptismal exhortation in the following way:

> The minister assures the congregation that when we ask anything of God it will be done for us, and then asks the members of the congregation to pray for the child. First, they are to pray that the child will be given faith, which is the gift of God's grace. Second, the congregation is to pray that our Lord himself baptize the child in water and in the Holy Spirit to the end that the outward washing, which God does through the minister, might be accomplished inwardly through the Holy Spirit.[10]

Typically, the traditonal baptismal sermon was from Matthew 19, Mark 10, or Luke 18, Jesus blessing the children. This was followed by a short exhortation to believe the words that have been read and to pray that the children may receive the kingdom and that they may receive the gift of faith by which they will become true children of God, heirs and fellow heirs with Christ.[11]

The baptismal exhortation became important with the rise of Anabaptism. An explanation of what was being done and the exact reasons for it came into sharper focus. As the appreciation for baptism deepened, the sermons became more elaborate. Pastors, however, exercised discretion, and one can discover a variety of baptismal exhortations for certain occasions.[12]

In Zwingli's *Basel Service Book of 1526,* a baptismal exhortation outlines the plan of salvation. He talks first about humanity's need for a Savior. Then he speaks in reference to Ephesians and the mystery of God's eternal plan of salvation revealed in Christ. He urges the people to pray for the child before them so that he or she may come to recognize Jesus Christ as Savior and be born again through the work of the Holy Spirit. The exhortation ends, "Let us pray that as we sacramentally through baptism add this child to the number of the faithful, he might also be received by our heavenly Father and be enrolled in the book of life."[13]

In 1524 the Swiss Anabaptist leader, Conrad Grebel (1498–1526), wrote to Thomas Muntzer (ca. 1488–1525), his German counterpart, indicating his group's intention to move from the practice of infant baptism to believers' baptism. The next year Balthasar Hubmaier, who shared Grebel's view, described his practice concerning infants:

> Instead of baptism, I have the church come together, bring the infant in, explain in German the gospel, "They brought little children" [Matt. 19:13]. When a name is given it, the whole church prays for the child on bended knees, and commends it to Christ, that he will be gracious and intercede for it.[14]

Seventeenth-century Puritan prayer books placed baptism immediately following the sermon. One of them implied that the exhortation was to be given with the Anabaptists in mind: "Neither is it requisite that all those that receyve this sacramente haue the vse of vnderstanding and faythe but chiefelye that they be conteyned vnder the name of gods people."[15]

The relationship between sixteenth-century Anabaptists and the English Baptists of the next century remains open.[16]

In the seventeenth century the practice of infant presentation and parental dedication was common among the English General Baptists but there is little evidence for a similar ceremony among the Calvinistic Baptists. Some eighteenth-century Baptists conducted a "Solemn Dedication" but there is uncertainty if this actually was a formal act of worship.[17]

Infant dedication was practiced among the Baptists of the American Colonies as early as 1774. Morgan Edwards (1722–1795) of the Philadelphia Baptist Association wrote, "The feeling of a need for infant dedication in Baptist churches in recent years seems to have developed in response to a desire for a rite similar to that of infant baptism as practiced in other Protestant churches."[18]

Sermons were included in baptismal services in the eighteenth century. Baptist Andrew Gifford of Eagle-Street Baptist Church, London, preached at an open-air baptism at Whittlesford, near Cambridge. The service included several "exhortations."[19] Particular Baptists were similar to other Calvinists, Independents, and Presbyterians when conducting baptisms. The service included praise, prayers, and the sermon.[20] English Methodist preachers were encouraged to "use [their] own judgment" when preaching at the baptism of children.[21]

American Puritans allowed a baptism sermon in their services. Cotton Mather (1663–1728) advised New England congregations:

> Some few, instead of this latter Prayer, do give the Parent's a brief Admonition to bring up their Children in the Nurture and Admonition of the Lord. Be sure, if an Adult Person be baptised, an Admonition, has sometimes, thought very agreeably to accompany the latter Prayer.[22]

John Clifford (1836–1932) was a distinguished Baptist pastor in England. He is credited with popularizing a "Dedication Service for Infants." At first the services of dedication were held in the home but were moved later to the church. Clifford was pastor of the cosmopolitan Praed Street Chapel in London. The church had people from Methodist and Congregationalist backgrounds who "desired a public service so that the members could take part in it."[23] A sermon may have been part of the service. Nineteenth-century American Baptist Russell H. Conwell (1843–1925) popularized an infant dedication ceremony, which included preaching in the context of worship.[24]

Today the act of baptism and preaching continue to be linked. Baptism in most Protestant worship is understood to be "a response to the proclamation of the Word."[25] The sermon either focuses on the baptism or alludes to it.[26] Preaching has had a prominent place in the practice of baptism. History shows it. As faithful preachers, we want to continue it.

The Theology of Baptism and Infant Presentation/Parental Dedication Sermons

Throughout the history of the church, preaching has been considered essential to the celebration of baptism. The sermon encourages worship, provides biblical instruction, gives moral teaching, and furnishes theological connections.

The act of baptism is a visible declaration of what God is doing in the lives of his people. Reformed Christians see baptism as the sign and seal of the covenant of grace.[27] Robert M. Shelton observes, "The sacraments have traditionally been understood and practiced as proclamation."[28] The sermon is "absolutely essential" to the sacrament.[29] The sermon is the time when the sacrament is explained and significance of the event celebrated. Calvin put it this way:

We ought to understand the word not as one whispered without meaning and without faith, a mere noise, like a magic incantation, which has the force to consecrate the element. Rather, it should, when preached, make us understand what the visible sign means.[30]

For Calvin and many ministers today, "the sacrament requires preaching to beget faith."[31]

The practice of infant presentation/parental dedication requires careful theological reflection.[32] The ceremony does not have a long history, and one minister says it is "a practice in need of a theology."[33] Believers' churches that observe infant dedication must get a firm grasp on what they are doing when conducting the ceremony. Where a minister lands theologically will influence the way he or she will preach.[34]

Sermons at a baptism or dedication ceremony, from the days of the early church to the present, can be classified either as an evangelistic/missionary sermon or an instructive sermon (nature of salvation, moral, doctrinal, meaning of baptism). These sermons contribute to defining the theology of baptism and practice of living as a disciple of Jesus Christ.

Baptism or a presentation/dedication is worship. The ceremony should not be an addendum but fit into the flow of the worship service. The act is a visible reminder of what living faith does. The Word preached affirms it.

Saying It Right in the Sermon

Baptism or a presentation/dedication ceremony usually takes place during a regular worship service. Occasionally for those who practice believers' baptism, services are held out of doors. Scripture is read. Songs are sung. A sermon is preached. God is worshiped. Preachers want to keep the Word and the act of baptism and presentation/dedication services connected. This requires that ministers have a firm understanding of theology, biblical exegesis, and their listeners.

If a preacher is committed to the above, he will have something to say that will make the event meaningful to the listeners and honoring to God. Garth Bolinger remarks:

> Pastoral words spoken and ministry given during the moments of baptism or dedication carry unusual weight. The infants are recipients. So are their parents. And the congregation not only hear the Story but become part of it as they bring children to Christ.[35]

The pastor must have clear thinking about his task and a heart for his people.

Linking with the Listeners

Baptism or dedication ceremonies are personal and call for more pastoral guidance than on other occasions. Vulnerable young Christian parents come to you to help them get started instructing their little one in the faith. They need you to help them understand what they are doing as they baptize or present their child. They know that you will conduct the ceremony and will preach, but they also need you to care.

A middle-aged woman has come to faith in Jesus Christ. She wants to be baptized. Her husband is not a Christian and is opposed to her newfound faith. She needs you not just to preach at her baptism but to care for her as she lives out her commitment to Christ.

Get to know the couple or the person being baptized. This is not easy for the busy pastor. If the pastor cannot do this, someone from the church needs to come alongside the parents or the candidate for baptism to answer questions and to give instruction. Try to involve the parents in the planning of the baptism or dedication service. Include the baptismal candidate's family in the preparation for baptism. As for other special services, ask questions about the faith of those involved and that of their families who will be attending. More often than not participants do not fully understand what is taking place at a baptism or dedication service. Family or friends who attend may be even less likely to know what is happening. Sometimes longtime church-goers are mistaken in their understanding of baptisms or infant dedications.

At one of the churches I served as pastor, a woman asked me if I would "do it" to her infant grandson. I said, "Do what?" She replied, "Dedicate him." Unfortunately neither parent was a believer. Still, she wanted me to "do it" to her grandson. I was able to talk with her about the reasons for infant presentation/parental dedication. Preachers must give thorough instruction about the nature of baptism and dedication in preparation for the service and in the sermon.

Preachers who recognize the pastoral dimension of baptism and dedication services will make connections with those involved. The connection will be seen in the sermon and ceremony. The pastoral care coupled with a biblical base will help the minister shape a sermon and ceremony that is God centered and audience aware.

A Baptism or Dedication Sermon Is Focused

The baptism or dedication sermon requires focus. Preachers need to ask themselves, Why am I giving *this* sermon at *this* occasion? Also the minister develops his purpose for preaching the sermon from a careful study of the following: the kind of ceremony (baptism or infant presentation/parental dedication), the setting (at the church building or out of doors; during a regular worship service), the parents (nature of their faith commitment), the baptismal candidate (his or her faith commitment), family and friends gathered (their faith commitment), and the congregation (their understanding of the ceremony).

The preacher develops a purpose statement that keeps in mind biblical and theological commitments, pastoral concerns, and audience needs. The purpose statement gives ministers a mark to hit when developing the sermon and may look like the following:

> As a result of hearing this sermon, my listeners [parents and congregation] will know the meaning of baptism.
>
> As a result of hearing this sermon, my listeners [parents and congregation] will be active in the nurture of the infant's life in Christ.
>
> As a result of hearing this sermon, my listeners [baptismal candidate and congregation] will live with praise to God for salvation in Christ.

Everything said in the sermon feeds into fulfilling the purpose.

A Baptism or Dedication Sermon Is Unique

There are patterns for baptism sermons that have been used throughout the centuries. Our task is to use the design but shape it into a central-idea sermon that is biblical and audience aware. Instead of using a stock sermon, ministers must build bridges from the sermon to the ceremony, making the event unique. A central idea can be developed as preachers keep in mind the uniqueness of *this* baptism or dedication, *these* parents, *this* baptismal candidate, or *this* congregation. A unique baptism or dedication sermon may have a central idea that is influenced by the following:

the theology of baptism/dedication
the evangelistic nature of baptism/dedication
repentance and baptism
instruction

- nature of salvation
- recounting of salvation history
- morality
- doctrine

a text that is the life verse or favorite verse of the parents/candidate

a text the pastor has chosen for the infant/parents/candidate

a text that reflects the personality of the infant/candidate

a text that captures the uniqueness of the infant/candidate as revealed by the meaning of his or her name

Some of the categories listed were emphases we discovered in our study of the baptism sermon in the early church: evangelistic (missionary preaching), repentance (penitential preaching), instructive (catechetical preaching); or the church of the Reformation: meaning of baptism (baptismal exhortation). The other possibilities include the selection of a text that is special for the persons involved on that occasion.

Baptism and presentation/dedication sermons bring together text and people. Try to select a text that will capture the meaning and moment of the ceremony. Familiar texts can be striking when developed with creativity. Unfamiliar passages may be meaningful because of their uniqueness. The preacher needs to find an angle of creativity and shape the sermon to the occasion and audience.

Baptisms and dedications are not all the same. Cookie-cutter sermons and ceremonies may tarnish the ceremony's significance for the parents, candidate, and congregation. The preacher must work with the text and the context and shape a sermon that makes a difference in the lives of those who celebrate with him.

A Baptism or Dedication Sermon Fits into the Worship Service

Baptisms or dedication ceremonies must fit into the flow of the worship service. They are not appendages. They are important life-giving events in the life of the church. When the ceremony is not an integral part of the worship service, the preacher may not mention the baptism or dedication even though it will take place later in the service. Little effort is made to connect the sermon and ceremony. Yet baptisms and dedications are significant events in the lives of the parents and candidates for baptism, and also in the life of the church. A responsible biblical and theological approach for ministers is to intentionally link the sermon and the ceremony. This helps to instruct the congregation.

When the baptism or dedication is part of the worship service, the minister needs to keep in mind the length of the sermon. The baptism or dedication should not be hurried, so the sermon should not be long. Usually the congregation expects a worship service to be long when a baptism or dedication is included. However, ministers should plan well for the service so that everyone involved may worship God well and not be concerned about a service that is too long. This is especially the case when a church has multiple services. If preachers have a clear idea, they will be able to preach clearly and concisely as they tie the sermon to the ceremony, without making the service too long.

Some baptisms are conducted outside the regular worship hour. A clear, brief baptism sermon will contribute to the celebration. I suggest a length of ten to fifteen minutes. The infant being baptized, the parents dedicating themselves to nurture their daughter in the faith, the young man who has embraced Christ as Savior are the focal point of the service. They are the visible story of God's work in their lives. Our role is to help them tell their story so that God may get all the credit.

A Baptism or Dedication Sermon Has a Clear Central Idea

Clarity is key in all preaching. It may be easy for ministers to choose a theologically thick text on which to preach. Baptism is not an easy doctrine to untangle. Be sure you are clear in your understanding of the text before you attempt to communicate it. Make sure the idea of the text is clear for yourself and for your listeners. The parents, candidate, and congregation may not understand what is taking place before their eyes. Preachers must wrestle with the text and occasion to help their listeners grasp what is going on. State the idea concisely. Express the idea in language the listeners can understand.

Listed earlier in the chapter are several ways preachers can shape the idea of a baptism or presentation/dedication sermon. One of my students preached an instructive baptism sermon based on a classic baptism text, Romans 6:1–11. Her subject question was, What did Paul tell the Roman Christians it means to be baptized into Christ Jesus? Her complement was, That believers are baptized into his death and a new life. The idea then became, Paul's telling the Roman Christians to be baptized into Christ Jesus means that believers are baptized into his death and a new life. Her homiletical idea was, Baptism is the outward sign of inner cleansing.

The sermon was written with a couple and their infant daughter in mind. The introduction of the sermon raised the need, What is this sacrament called baptism? The sermon moved from there, making connections throughout from the text to the couple, to the child, to the congregation. She used the occasion to teach.[36]

Haddon Robinson takes the angle of moral instruction for Romans 6 in his homiletical idea, You are not the person you used to be, so you can never live life as you used to live it.

The parents of the child being baptized or dedicated or the candidate for baptism may have a life verse or a favorite passage of Scripture read at the service. The Coopermans chose Romans 8:26–27:

> In the same way, the Spirit helps us in our weakness. We do not know what we ought to pray for, but the Spirit himself intercedes for us with groans that words cannot express. And he who searches our hearts knows the mind of the Spirit, because the Spirit intercedes for the saints in accordance with God's will.

This is not a typical baptism passage, but the student who preached this sermon wove together well the text and the occasion. Her homiletical idea was, In the language of prayer, the Spirit is our interpreter. She stated in the second section of the sermon,

> And we will have the privilege today of calling upon that interpreter as we baptize little Carrie Cooperman. Carrie's parents are here today as faithful Christians who want to raise their daughter to know and love Jesus Christ. As faithful believers in Christ, they have been given the gift of the Spirit through their own baptisms.

The idea was stated clearly and developed throughout the sermon.[37] The key for preachers is to know what the text is saying and then intersect it with the occasion to create a clear idea.

Preaching the Sermon

Ministers would do well to keep in mind the following when preaching for the baptism/dedication service:

Cultivate a sense of joy
Get and maintain eye contact with the parents, candidate, and congregation
Be warm, compassionate, and friendly
Watch body language and tone of voice
Repeat the homiletical idea at least three times
Be conversational
Articulate, and project your voice
Know the names of the parents and child
Know the name of the baptismal candidate
Be brief

Try to preach without notes. You will want to have worked on an outline and a manuscript. Become familiar with the flow of the sermon in order to communicate clearly and naturally. You do not want to memorize your manuscript. Instead, become familiar with the flow of the outline. If you leave something out, only you will know it! Preaching without notes means that you are not shooting from the hip but that you have prepared well.

Some parts of the list are the same for other special services, but a few features need to be emphasized here. Baptism and dedication services are moments of celebration, therefore pastors should cultivate a sense of joy. Baptism and dedications normally happen once, so pastors need to make the occasion meaningful by their words and presence.

Know the names of the parents/infant/candidate for baptism. Make sure you know how to pronounce the name correctly. Check with the parents or persons involved. Write the name down phonetically if you are unfamiliar with its pronunciation.

If preaching out of doors, articulate and project your voice. Try to be conversational and not force your voice by straining it or sounding like you are shouting.

Be clear about the homiletical idea. Listeners must get it. Repeat it and restate it. Baptisms and dedication sermons are a challenge to the preacher to capture the wonder of the event into a single sentence that feeds the lives of the listeners.

Practicing to Preach

1. Select one of these sources for shaping a baptism/dedication sermon: the theology of baptism, a great baptism text, a text that intersects with the experience of the parents or person being baptized, a text that reflects the personality of the parents or person being baptized, texts that capture the uniqueness of the candidate for baptism by using his or her name.
2. Find the subject, complement, and idea for the text.
3. List the images and repeated words or phrases found in the text.
4. List the characteristics of the person being baptized or the parents, and the congregation. How should the ceremony be affected by these characteristics?
5. Write a purpose statement: As a result of hearing this baptism sermon, my listeners [parents/candidate and congregation] will . . .
6. Write a homiletical idea.
7. Write a sermon outline.
8. Write a sermon manuscript.

Shelf-Wise ────────────────

Berkley, James D., ed. *Leadership Handbooks of Practical Theology.* Vol. 1, *Word & Worship.* Grand Rapids: Baker, 1995.

Bolinger, Garth. "Infant Rites," *Leadership* 8, no. 4 (fall 1987): 116–21.

Chapell, Bryan. *Christ-Centered Preaching: Redeeming the Expository Sermon.* Grand Rapids: Baker, 1997.

Shelley, Marshall, ed. *Changing Lives through Preaching and Worship.* Nashville: Moorings, 1995.

West, W. M. S. "The Child and the Church: A Baptist Perspective." In *Pilgrim Pathways: Essays in Baptist History in Honor of B. R. White.* Edited by William H. Brackney and Paul S. Fiddes with John H. Y. Briggs. Macon: Mercer University Press, 1999: 75–110.

5

Preaching at the Celebration of the Lord's Supper

The preacher must guide the listener through the sermon to celebrate the Supper.

Preaching at the Lord's Supper can be challenging. The time allotted to the sermon may be less than normal. The occasion may be observed frequently or infrequently in the life of a congregation, each tradition presenting its own difficulties. Some preachers make no effort to build a bridge between the sermon and the Supper. Some have fallen into a routine and have given up helping listeners make sense of what is going on.

Some churches feel that the Supper is an ordinance of the *church* to be celebrated at a church service. The theological position on the Lord's Supper needs to be taken into consideration when planning when and where to celebrate it.

I have preached at communion services during morning worship services, at training conferences, and at church camp. Each time I have tried to capture in my preaching the power of Christ's love for sinners as celebrated in the Supper. The celebration of the Lord's Supper is vitally linked to preaching: The Supper is a visible demonstration of the preached Word.

The History of the Lord's Supper Sermon

The celebration of the Supper is rooted in the Jewish Passover Seder. The Seder is a home service on the first and second nights of the Passover. It dramatizes in word and symbolic act the story of the Jewish exodus from Egypt. Even during the days of the temple, Passover was observed in homes. However, the main celebration took place in Jerusalem. People from out of town and locals attended the temple service and shared the paschal meal. They took their instructions from Exodus 12:8: "That same night they are to eat the meat roasted over the fire, along with bitter herbs, and bread made without yeast."

After the temple was destroyed, the paschal lamb was eliminated from the Seder. Other elements were transferred to the home. The meal was instructive, an "exposition of the Exodus story,"[1] teaching generations about God's deliverance.[2] The homilies and other basic elements of the Seder are shaped by the deliverance motif.[3] The Seder service includes a Mishnaic homily summarizing the historic events from Abraham to enslavement. This is followed by a running commentary on each word in Deuteronomy 26:5–8.[4]

By the middle ages, preaching also took place on the Sabbath before Passover, "the Great Sabbath." Some sermons addressed the details of the laws governing the observance while others examined major themes of the celebration and its liturgy.[5] The pattern continued through the eighteenth century.[6] The modern Jewish and messianic Seder provides for a homily.[7]

The early church held two services on the Lord's Day: in the morning, when the Scriptures were read and preached and in the evening, at which the Lord's Supper was celebrated. Both services had a sermon.[8]

By the end of the first century the Eucharist was no longer observed in the evening.[9] In the second century Justin Martyr mentions the Supper twice in *First Apology* (ca. 155). In the first instance (ch. 65) it was preceded by baptism, in the second (ch. 67) by the liturgy of the Word. On Sunday a reading was taken from "the memoirs of the apostles or the writings of the prophets . . . as long as time permits." Following the reading "the president in a discourse urges and invites [us] to the imitation of these noble things."[10]

John Chrysostom (ca. 347–407), Theodore of Mopsuestia (ca. 350–428), Cyril of Jerusalem (ca. 315–386), Ambrose (339–397), and Augustine (354–430) model in their sermons preaching linked to the celebration of the Supper.[11] Augustine spoke of the importance of the Word being connected to the sacrament.[12]

By the end of the fifth century the Mass, or the liturgy of the Eucharist, was conceived.[13] The medieval period emphasized the Mass and diminished preaching. The Mass was considered the normal way of celebrating public worship. The act itself was thought to be preaching.[14]

Some groups continued preaching during the medieval period. An early Dominican priest, Guillaume de Peyraut (ca. 1190–1271), addressed the Christian's worthiness of receiving communion.[15] German mystic and Dominican John Tauler (ca. 1300–1361) touched on the spiritual use of holy communion. However, Tauler's sermons tended to depart from Scripture soon after they began.[16]

At the time of the Reformation, Martin Luther proposed "a short, appropriate Order for Baptism and the Sacrament and everything centered on the Word and Prayer and Love."[17] He suggested, "Since the chief and greatest aim of any Service is to preach and teach God's Word," Sundays would have three sermons: early, at the Mass, and at Vespers.[18] Luther put preaching and the Lord's Supper back together.

Martin Bucer, John Calvin, and John Knox likewise wed the sermon and the Supper. Bucer's Strassburg Liturgy states, "Near the end of the Sermon, the Minister explains the action of the Lord's Supper and exhorts the people to observe the same with right faith and true devotion."[19] Calvin similarly wrote, "On the day of the Lord's Supper, the Minister touches upon it in the conclusion of his Sermon, or better, if there is occasion, preaches the whole sermon about it, in order to explain to the people what our Lord wishes to say and signify by this mystery, and in what way it behooves us to receive it."[20] Knox's prayer book includes an exhortation.[21]

English Congregationalists kept the sermon and Supper together. The church of pastor and hymnwriter Isaac Watts (1674–1748), Bury Street Independent Meeting in London, celebrated the Lord's Supper on the first Sunday of the month during the afternoon service:

> The Lord's Supper is administered alternately by the two pastors in the plainest manner, just according to the institution, first the history of the institution is read, either out of Matthew's gospel or the first ep. Corinthians, that it may ever be kept in mind to regulate every part of the practice; and the sermons of that day being equally suited to the design of the Lord's Supper, or a commemoration of the sufferings of Christ, 'tis but seldom any other speech or exhortation is made before the celebration.[22]

American Puritan Cotton Mather (1663–1728) describes how the Lord's Supper was practiced in New England churches:

When the LORD'S SUPPER is to be administrated, the *Pastor* gives Notice of it a week before hand. And when the *Lord's Day* for it arrives, he usually accommodates the solemn Occasion before him, with a Sermon upon some agreeable *Doctrine of the Gospel*.[23]

The sermon and the Supper are held together. English Methodists conducted quarterly "Love-Feasts," where they celebrated a ceremony similar to the Lord's Supper. In this case, they ate bread and water. The preacher began the service with singing and extemporaneous prayer. Then individuals gave testimony to their Christian experience.[24] When some churches decided to conduct the Lord's Supper, they did according "to the form of the church of England: though some of the preachers deviate from it a little; no strict uniformity is insisted upon, but every one is allowed to use his own judgment."[25]

Several nineteenth-century movements emphasized a return to the "primitive church." Following the Oxford Movement, these included the Primitive Methodists (1812), the Plymouth Brethren (1827), the Catholic Apostolic Church (1835), the Disciples of Christ (1833 in U.S., 1843 in Britain), and the Salvation Army (1865). Most of these groups insisted on the celebration of communion each Lord's Day.[26] The Primitive Methodist service began with a "brief address" followed by a brief exhortation, hymns, prayers, and the Supper.[27] Plymouth Brethren observed open communion and the preaching of the Word or "Bible Reading."[28] The founder of the Plymouth Brethren, John N. Darby (1800–1882), wrote, "We take the Lord's Supper every Sunday, and those who have the gift for it preach the Gospel of salvation or good of his neighbor according to the capacity which God has given him."[29] Later in the nineteenth century, Charles Haddon Spurgeon (1834–1892), among others, preached at the Lord's Supper.[30]

Since the time of the 1549 Anglican Prayer Book, a sermon or homily has been required at the Eucharist.[31] Methodists continue the practice of preaching at the Lord's Supper:

> Preaching is fully as important on communion Sundays as on other occasions. The omission of preaching on communion Sundays violates the unity of Word and Sacrament. This does not mean that it is necessary to preach on the subject of Holy Communion every time it is celebrated; any facet of the gospel can be preached in such a way that it leads appropriately to the celebration of Holy Communion.[32]

There is reason that the sermon should be connected to the celebration of the Lord's Supper. Preaching gives meaning to the observance. The ordinance gains its power from the Word.

The Theology of Lord's Supper Sermons

Preachers need a theology of the sermon and the Supper. Their theology should drive the preaching. "As the Reformers knew, Word and Sacrament belong together," says William Willimon.[33] However, some disagree. Ozora S. Davis argued, "The sacrament itself seldom, if ever, calls for a sermon." He continued, "Indeed, a formal discourse hardly fits its celebration."[34] The Catholic tradition and some Protestant higher church traditions may view the celebration of the Supper as *the* sermon—what is done in the partaking of the bread and the cup is sermon enough. No other words are necessary. However, most Protestants see the celebration of the Supper and the preaching of a sermon as inseparable. Objections to linking the sermon and Supper may come from one's theology of the Supper itself.

The perspective of this book is that biblical preaching strives to join the two.[35] The sermon serves as the interpreter of the Supper. Preaching specifically on the Lord's Supper or concluding a sermon that connects the text with holy communion helps listeners recognize that the celebration is a fitting response to the Good News. John Calvin put it this way:

> [T]he right administering of the Sacrament cannot stand apart from the Word. For whatever benefit may come to us from the Supper requires the Word: whether we are to be confirmed in faith, or exercised in confession, or aroused to duty, there is need of preaching.[36]

Saying It Right in the Sermon

The sermon and the communion service should be done with thought and excellence. William Willimon urges preachers, "While our preaching may be a bit shorter on Communion Sundays, we should save our best sermons for these Sundays in order to underscore our belief in the linkage of the Word and Table."[37]

The Lord's Supper is often celebrated during a regular worship service. Occasionally it is observed at a vespers service, on Maundy Thursday, at conferences, or at camp firesides. Some denominations practice the sacrament weekly. At every observance, ministers must work at connecting the sermon with the celebration. The preaching must be clear, biblical, theologically relevant, and listener oriented.

Linking with Listeners

Familiarity can breed contempt, and familiarity can make some exempt. Just because people participate in the Supper does not mean that they understand what they are doing. The minister needs to find out the listeners' questions, concerns, and perceptions about holy communion and then address them. It is important to do this as often as the Supper is celebrated. Questions will vary. A newly converted seventeen-year-old asks, "What does it mean to participate in the Lord's Supper?" A father wonders, "Is it all right for my children to share in holy communion?" A seeker questions, "What is going on?"

The text may raise questions in listener's minds. The setting may too. Listeners will react to the presentation of the elements, the order of the service, and the mood of the service. I recall serving communion for the first time at my first pastorate. Early Sunday morning I went to the church building to see if everything was in order for the service. When I entered the sanctuary, I noticed a table at the front with a large white cloth the size of a sheet draped over the elements. My first thought was, *Who died?* The table looked like a coffin. I had a quick history lesson on why the church practiced the Supper this way. When I preached I reminded the listeners why, too.

Preachers who understand the importance of explanation will help their congregation. They will listen for their questions. Then, both preacher and people will be better worshipers.

A Communion Sermon Is Focused

Preachers constantly need to ask, Why *this* sermon at *this* time and on *this* occasion? The question may be answered differently depending on whether holy communion is observed quarterly, monthly, or weekly. The minister will have to determine where in the sermon the focus on the Supper will take place. The emphasis on the Supper may be the thrust of the sermon. Or the convergence may take place in the conclusion of the sermon. David L. Larsen suggests, "If we move into the service of Holy Communion, the conclusion must be established solidly."[38] The conclusion is the transition to the celebration of the Lord's Supper. The listeners need to see the bridge between the sermon and the Supper.

Ministers may use the standard lectionary or preach through a book of the Bible. In either case the preacher must intersect the text with the Supper. This can be done by developing a purpose for preaching the sermon. Preachers should consider their theological understanding of the Lord's Supper, the text, the setting (weekly, monthly, quarterly, Maundy Thursday, evening, camp, etc., and the layout of the elements), and the congregation (their questions, concerns, and faith commitment) when determining their purpose.

A purpose statement may look like the following:

> As a result of hearing this sermon, my listeners [congregation] will understand why we celebrate the Lord's Supper.
>
> As a result of hearing this sermon, my listeners [congregation] will celebrate their life in Jesus Christ.
>
> As a result of hearing this sermon, my listeners [camp participants] will appreciate their connection to other believers in Jesus Christ.

The purpose statement provides focus for the preacher in communicating to the listeners the aim of the celebration of the Supper.

A Communion Sermon Is Unique

The celebration of the Lord's Supper has a rich history. For centuries Christians have joined together in worship to break bread and drink the cup. Each time Christians gather, the event is a new reminder of an old reality. One challenge with preaching and communion is in its frequency. A congregation may celebrate the Supper weekly, monthly, or quarterly. No matter how often the Lord's Supper is observed, preachers may find it difficult to make each sermon and service different.

As I have said, the Lord's Supper may be celebrated while preaching through a book of the Bible, at the end of a week of family camp, or at a nursing home service. Whatever the occasion it can be linked to the text and the listeners. The wise preacher uses these elements to shape the sermon idea.

A unique Lord's Supper sermon may have a central idea that is influenced by the following:

the theology of the Lord's Supper
conversion and the Lord's Supper
instruction
  • nature of salvation
  • doctrine
  • limits and restrictions at the Lord's table
traditional texts used for the Lord's Supper
connection of the text with the Lord's Supper developed
  in the sermon's conclusion

A sermon that clearly articulates the theology of the Lord's Supper is always beneficial, as it reminds the participants of why they participate. Tim Keller of Redeemer Presbyterian Church in New York City says about the Lord's Supper, "I don't think there's any more effective way to help a person do a spiritual inventory."[39] It is the preacher's job to guide the congregation into the process of soul searching. Some people may even be challenged to come to faith by seeing believers share in the Lord's Supper.

Sermons can also be made unique by instructing listeners about the nature of salvation or focusing on a doctrinal aspect of holy communion or by examining the limits and restrictions at the Lord's table. In addition, traditional texts used for the Lord's Supper can be employed and shaped with the occasion and listeners in mind. A final way to make a communion sermon unique is to connect the text with the Lord's Supper at the conclusion of the sermon.

Although the practice of the Lord's Supper is repeatedly the same, not all sermons on the Lord's Supper need to be. Preachers must work hard at making each celebration unique yet connected to a distinguished past.

A Communion Sermon Fits into the Flow of Worship

Preachers need to be like good interior designers: They need to know how to arrange the service so that the sermon and Supper complement each other. William Willimon says, "A wise pastor will try to fit the Lord's Supper into the pattern and style of Sunday worship of the congregation."[40]

Preachers need to be aware of their congregation's attitude toward the Lord's Supper. Some congregations may not be comfortable with celebrating the Supper and this may affect how the pastor treats the ordinance. One pastor confessed that he has preached a sermon on communion only once in five years. He avoids talking about communion by placing an insert in the bulletin that explains the meaning of the service.[41] This may be what his congregation prefers, but a less educated congregation may be intimidated by printed material. Furthermore, this pastor is missing an opportunity: Explaining what is being done and why it is being done allows a congregation to worship together as one body.

Most communion celebrations take place during the regular worship service. Those who celebrate the Supper weekly are more used to a communion sermon and the length of the service than those who observe communion less often. Either way, worshipers should not get the impression that the Lord's Supper is an add-on to the worship service. That is why the transition from sermon to Supper is so important. Move from the sermon to the Supper by applying the theme of the worship service or the idea of the sermon. Use music (whether solo, group, choir, or congregational singing), responsive readings, or any other worship resource to aid listeners as they consider the connection between the sermon and the celebration of the Supper. (See the example in the next section.)

A Communion Sermon Has a Clear Central Idea

I have made the case for connecting the sermon with the Lord's Supper. This bridge helps listeners understand the observance and its connection with the text. Use texts that capture the meaning of the ceremony. Texts from the lectionary or in a series through a book need to be understood in light of the listeners and occasion.

The Lord's Supper is packed with theological factors that can confuse listeners. The ceremony itself does not explain to the listener what is taking place. The preacher must guide the listener through the sermon to celebrate the Supper. Among other factors this requires a clear central idea.

A sermon may be instructive. One of my students preached a communion sermon from Luke 24:13–35. The purpose was, As a result of hearing this sermon my listeners will understand that as we "do this in remembrance," we see Christ and ourselves from the perspective of God's plan and we remember that Jesus walks with us along life's way. The homiletical idea was, There is eye-opening truth in the breaking of bread.[42] The subject question was, What did the disciples learn as they gathered at the table in Emmaus? The complement was, They saw Jesus and themselves with greater perspective and realized that Jesus was always with them. The idea was, The disciples learned as they gathered at the table in Emmaus that they saw Jesus and themselves with greater perspective, and they realized that Jesus was always with them.

Another student preached from the text from the eleventh Sunday of Cycle C of the Common Lectionary, Luke 7:36–50 (short form). The subject question was, How does the sinful woman's response to Jesus' forgiveness differ from that of Simon the Pharisee? The complement was, Having been forgiven of many sins, she reponds with greater acts of love. Putting the subject and complement together the main idea was, The sinful woman's response to God's forgiveness differs from Simon the Pharisee's in that because she has been forgiven many sins, she responds with greater acts of love. The homiletical idea was, Our response to God's forgiveness should be shown in great acts of love. The purpose was, As a result of hearing this sermon the listeners will understand that as they "do this in remembrance" they see Christ and themselves in perspective of "God's plan" and they "remember" that Jesus walks with them along the way. The transition to the Supper was made in the conclusion:

> In celebrating the Communion meal, we acknowledge that Jesus died on the cross as the sacrifice for all our sin, and that death could not keep him in the grave, but that He is risen and lives now in the Kingdom of God, and He will come again to take us home. An incredible price was paid that you and I could be forgiven for all our sin—great and small. And what is your response going to be? Our response to his gift of forgiveness should be great acts of love.[43]

Preaching the Sermon

Keep in mind the following when preaching the communion sermon:

Create a sense of celebration
Connect the sermon with the Supper
Be friendly
Repeat the homiletical idea at least three times
Be conversational
Articulate, and project your voice
Preach without notes
Be brief

The above list gives reminders for all special services. One additional feature bears mention: Be careful to project the appropriate mood of the occasion. Pastors and worshipers often treat the Lord's Supper like a funeral and not a celebration of Christ's victory over death. We remember Maundy Thursday but forget about the Sunday evening meal at Emmaus.

When actually celebrating the Supper, make sure to project your voice. Sometimes sound equipment is not available. Determine to communicate the homiletical idea, which brings everything together as believers feed by faith on the Word and the Supper.

Practicing to Preach _____

1. Select one of the approaches to shaping a sermon on the Lord's Supper: the theology of the Supper; conversion and the Lord's Supper; instruction on the

nature of salvation, a doctrinal aspect of the Supper, the meaning of the Lord's Supper, or the limits and restrictions at the Lord's table; traditional texts used for the Lord's Supper; connection of the text with the Lord's Supper developed in the sermon's conclusion.
2. Find the subject, complement, and idea for the text.
3. List the images and repeated words or phrases found in the text.
4. List the theological characteristics regarding the Lord's Supper of the denomination or the congregation. How should the ceremony be affected by these characteristics?
5. Write a purpose statement: As a result of hearing this sermon/sermon on the Lord's Supper, my listeners [congregation] will . . .
6. Write a homiletical idea.
7. Write a sermon outline.
8. Write a sermon manuscript.

Shelf-Wise

Hybels, Bill, Stuart Briscoe, and Haddon Robinson. *Mastering Contemporary Preaching.* Portland: Multnomah Press, 1989.

Jacks, G. Robert. *Getting the Word Across: Speech Communication for Pastors and Lay Leaders.* Grand Rapids: Eerdmans, 1995.

Jacks, G. Robert. *Just Say the Word Across: Writing for the Ear.* Grand Rapids: Eerdmans, 1996.

Larsen, David L. *The Anatomy of Preaching: Identifying the Issues in Preaching Today.* Grand Rapids: Kregel, 1989.

6

Speaking
on Other Occasions

Special occasions in our communities become prime occasions to interject a timely word for God.

Cal LeMon

Ministers are asked to speak at all kinds of services or occasions.[1] They talk to the local Rotary
Club; they speak at the church missionary ban-
quet. Preachers give evangelistic series, baccalaureate sermons, and commencement addresses, and give
a word at the dedication of the monument in the town
square.

All occasions require preparation. Unfortunately some
of the special events interrupt the weekly routine of pastoral life. Each time the minister speaks, he or she needs to
decide what to say and how to say it. He or she must know
to whom it will be said. The principles of shaping a sermon

for the special occasions covered in this book will serve preachers anytime.

Principles to Keep in Mind

Listed below are elements to keep in mind when preparing to speak at various special events.

Understand the Occasion

Speakers need to ask themselves, Why *this* speech or sermon or address at *this* time on *this* occasion? First, preachers need to know the type of people to whom they are going to speak: their age, the size of the audience, their educational background, gender, and expertise. Second, preachers need to know the type of event at which they are speaking: the purpose of the event, expectations the hosts have for the speaker, the place where the event is held, the mood of the event, and the time allotted to the speaker.

Be Focused

A clear speech or sermon has a focus. Once the audience and occasion have been determined, the purpose statement can be made. Remember to make it the bull's eye of where the speech is to go. Be specific in the outcomes expected. A purpose statement disciplines the speaker and gives direction to the message.

Make the Speech Unique

Every occasion is different. Every sermon, speech, or address needs to be different too. The occasion and audience require it. Creativity is looking at things from a different angle. Warren W. Wiersbe urges, "Tie every 'special occasion' message to the Word of God and the heart of the occasion."[2]

Speeches are similar to the special preaching occasions we discussed earlier. Each one is different. Like a good physician, the speaker wants to make the right diagnosis of the occasion in which she is speaking and prescribe the appropriate medicine. An after-dinner talk at the evening Rotary Club that has a heavy dose of humor is easier for listeners to digest than a heavy speech jammed with facts and figures. You want to communicate information tailored to your audience and occasion.

Have a Central Idea

A central idea is a must for clarity. An ancient Greek speech advisor wrote, "Clarity of style must be a particular concern for the speaker throughout."[3] The central idea will give the speech, sermon, or address a unity that is often missing in speeches and sermons.

"Having a central idea tends to build unity into a speech," writes Duane Litfin, "allowing us to work in conjunction with the natural tendencies of our listeners' minds."[4] In addition Litfin writes, "A central idea within a speech promotes not only unity, but order and progress as well."[5] These three elements—unity, order, and progress— give a speech, sermon, or address direction. Joined with a clear purpose, a speech with a central idea will be clear.[6]

Make sure the idea is stated at least three times, if not more, throughout the speech. Be creative. Make it crisp and memorable. Think of the central idea as the lozenge you place in your listeners' mouths. They leave the event sucking on the idea and savoring the strength of its truth.

Creating a memorable central idea takes work. No one is a pro at it immediately. But the work is worth it as you experience the pleasure of your listeners remembering what you said and how you said it.

Rob Peter to Pay Paul

There can be as many as three different preparations a week for a minister: a Sunday morning sermon, Sunday evening sermon, and possibly a midweek Bible study or sermon. How can preachers possibly add another speaking engagement to their calendars? My answer is, Borrow—or even steal! When preparing for a speech for the missionary society or the dedication of the town cemetery, be a Robin Hood: Take from the riches of your study for the sermons or Bible study for that week. Give it to the poor—the special occasion—whether it is an after-dinner speech, a town event, or even a funeral, wedding, or baptism.

Preachers who know how to get the most out of their study will do double duty with their work. Research for one sermon can be used in a Bible study, a speech, or a devotional. They will be less stressed too. Instead of relying on surface research, they can study one or two areas more deeply. The result is stronger sermons and speeches.

When Duane Litfin was a pastor in Memphis, he preached from the same text on Sunday mornings and evenings. Sunday morning focused often on the explanation or proof of the text. The evening sermon explored application more fully. Litfin is a good example of making the most of study.[7] Listeners benefit from the fuller treatment and deeper exegesis of texts. Preachers benefit by not having to come up with "new material."

The lesson for the busy preacher is this: When preparing for extra speaking engagements, preachers have permission to break the eighth commandment. Steal, borrow, and stretch from what you already have. Use illustrations from other preachers, books, and articles.

Build Resources

Gather material for your illustration files for various occasions. Be vigilant at collecting articles, quotations, stories, jokes, and other items that may be used in any number of occasions. Warren Wiersbe offers sage advice: "Never allow a good text to slip through your fingers."[8] When preparing for a sermon or reading the Bible devotionally, a text might strike you as appropriate for a particular special occasion. Write down the reference and file it. Most preachers know this but fail to practice it—careful collecting now will pay off in the future.

Occasions to Consider

The purpose of this section is to understand the unique considerations for each of the special occasions mentioned earlier in the chapter.

Evangelistic Services

The intent of evangelistic preaching is to persuade listeners to change their minds about Jesus Christ. Myron Augsburger observes, "An evangelistic sermon will clarify the gospel and highlight its uniqueness in the world today."[9] Preachers should winsomely challenge their audience with the gospel. Some listeners will be willing to hear what we have to say while others will be defensive. We need to understand our listeners and construct a sermon that will target their souls.[10]

Several things must be kept in mind when putting together an evangelistic sermon. First, an evangelistic sermon should be biblical. Say what the Bible says, what that particular text says. Ask yourself *What does the text reveal of the human situation?*[11] Anticipate and answer questions and objections the listeners might have about the text.

Second, an evangelistic sermon should be simple. Men and women should know the preacher's point—the idea. The strengths of an evangelistic sermon are simplicity and clarity. Robert Coleman says this about the evangelistic sermon: "A well-prepared sermon will be uncomplicated in its basic organization and language (2 Corinthians 11:3)."[12]

Third, evangelistic sermons have a sense of urgency. They are fueled by the evangelist's conviction that what he or she has to say is a matter of life and death. The preacher's passion will be felt by the listeners. Preachers want to be genuine. "Be sincere when you relate the urgent demands of the gospel," says Bryan Chapell, "and trust God to use what you truly feel along with the truth of his Word to melt skepticism."[13]

The After-Dinner Speech

The after-dinner speech is an American custom. It developed from the "toast" in England. The Romans used a piece of toasted bread dipped in wine when they pledged the health of their guests. Legend has it that in medieval times the "loving cup" was passed with a piece of toast in it. When emptied the host would drink the dregs and eat the piece of toast in honor of the guests.[14]

In England the custom grew. It started with a "toast" to the woman who was the belle of the gathering, or to several women in turn. The one who proposed the toast would raise his cup, offer the name of the woman as the "toast," and drink in her honor. A brief statement was made by the host and the people would drink.[15]

There are obvious disadvantages to after-dinner speaking. First, there is the time. The food sits in the stomach, the eyelids get heavy, the body finds it tough to listen and would rather fall off to sleep. Second, there are expectations. Since the body is ready to shut down, the listener expects the speaker to be especially interesting and entertaining. *I dare you to keep me awake!* thinks the listener. These two factors alone are enough for an after-dinner speaker to admit defeat.

Wage war against time and expectations in these ways: Be light (humorous), relate to life, be short, be lively, use human interest, and tell stories. One of my students put these principles into practice in an after-dinner speech on fly-fishing. His subject question was, Why should I take up fly-fishing? His complement was, Because it's a refreshing and relaxing way to ease the stress of life. The idea was, You should take up fly-fishing because it's a refreshing and relaxing way to ease the stress of life. For his after-dinner audience, he expressed his idea in this catchy sentence: If there are knots in your line, chances are there aren't knots in your life.

His speech was humorous. He began, "I am no different than any angler; I love to tell fish stories." He related the speech to life: "Just as rubbing the belly of your hunting dog soothes him, fly-fishing settles and soothes me like few things can." The speech was only about ten minutes. He told it in a lively way, filled with human interest and snippets of stories. By the end, we all wanted to take up fly-fishing![16]

The Dedication or Community Event Speech

Community celebrations, patriotic events, building dedications, mortgage burnings, and other occasions outside the daily routine require imagination, focus, and sensitivity. A pastor friend of mine was asked to speak at the dedication of the town flagpole. What does one say about a flagpole? He decided to emphasize the foundation of the flagpole. The pole towered above the crowd. Although the people could not see the substructure, it was anchored by six tons of concrete. He urged that the moral foundation of the community and nation be as solid as the foundation that bears the symbol. He used the occasion creatively to reflect the convictions he represents as a pastor.

You, as a pastor, may think that you shouldn't be involved in community events, but your presence there is vital. "A preacher will proclaim the gospel in his community in terms of who he is," observes Chevis F. Horne. "Being is as important as saying and doing."[17] Ministers may feel uncomfortable speaking at community or patriotic functions, but as Cal LeMon urges, "even though our communities often see us as pallid stand-ins for an absentee God, we can seize these public platforms to play out grace."[18]

The Baccalaureate Sermon and Commencement Address

Typically graduations have had two events: the baccalaureate service and commencement ceremony. When I was a pastor, the local ministerial association sponsored the baccalaureate service for the local high school. Most of the graduating students attended the event with their families. The sermon was delivered by a local pastor. Today many communities have stopped hosting high school baccalaureate services because of their religious content, but Christian schools still have these services.

James D. Berkley urges baccalaureate speakers to be Christian, contemporary, personal, focused, and brief.[19] Berkley's list is helpful for both baccalaureate sermons and commencement addresses. He says, "A single focus . . . may be remembered, whereas a generic worship service in praise of God or a service that tries to cover the full sweep of the gospel will be left scattered on the floor with the bulletins."[20]

Frederick D. Kershner kept focus in one of his commencement addresses, "The Life Worth While." His speech led up to the idea, Without God no life truly worthwhile can be lived; with him such a life may easily become a glorious reality.[21] Likewise, in the baccalaureate sermon, "The Trust of Dedicated Personality," Harold W. Reed underscored the single idea, Dedicated men change the world.[22]

Time is a factor at any occasion, but brevity at graduation exercises is a virtue. At Western Maryland College for the last twenty years the faculty has run a gambling pool based on how long the graduation exercise will last![23] It seems to keep getting longer and longer. Likewise, students "endure commencement speakers as the final indignity of an educative process that has trapped them for more years than they care to remember."[24] A word of advice: Match the length of the speech with the attention span of the listeners. We can assume that students about to graduate will not be attentive for long.

The baccalaureate sermon or commencement address are opportunities given "to the preacher to sound the call to service with the voice of a herald."[25] Make the sermon or speech relevant and inspire the audience with your words.

Practicing to Speak or Preach _____

1. Select one of the special occasions listed above. Analyze your audience.
2. Find the subject and complement for an idea for the speech or text.
3. List the images or elements that signify the event.
4. Write a purpose statement: As a result of hearing this speech, my listeners will . . .
5. Write a homiletical idea.
6. Write an outline.
7. Write a manuscript.

Shelf-Wise _____

Chilson, Richard W. *Evangelization Homily Hints: A Resource for Catholic Preachers.* New York/Mahwah, N.J.: Paulist Press, 2000.

Loscalzo, Craig A. *Evangelistic Preaching That Connects: Guidance in Shaping Fresh and Appealing Sermons.* Downers Grove: InterVarsity Press, 1995.

Perry, Lloyd M., and John Strabhar. *Evangelistic Preaching.* Chicago: Moody, 1979.

Stanfield, V. L. *Effective Evangelistic Preaching.* Grand Rapids: Baker 1965.

APPENDIX 1

Special-Occasion Sermon Worksheet

Occasion:

Text:

Subject:

Complement:

Idea:

Purpose: As a result of hearing this sermon, my listeners
will . . .

Mood of the text:

Mood of the occasion:

Person/s:

Particulars:

Appendix 2

Ten Commandments for Funeral Messages

Excerpted from Earl Daniels, *The Funeral Message* (Nashville: Cokesbury, 1937), 103–8.

I. Thou shalt not bear false witness.

Tell the truth—not necessarily the whole truth, but nothing but the truth. You do not need to take out the family skeleton and rattle its bones in the presence of the assembled multitude. But neither do you need to bring out the ministerial whitewash.

II. Thou shalt remember that sympathy will cover a multitude of homiletical sins.

There is no substitute for it. If people feel that you really care for them, and that you feel the burden of their sorrow, they will overlook a lot of mistakes.

III. Thou shalt not be heard for thy much speaking.

A short, simple message is more fitting than a long-winded oratory.

IV. Thou shalt beware of deathbed stories.

Your function as a minister is to make it easier rather than more difficult for the family to face their loss.

V. Thou shalt fit the message to the occasion.

The same suit will not fit every man. Neither will the same funeral message. Let there be such individuality about the sermon as there is in made-to-measure clothes.

VI. Thou shalt not cry with a loud voice.

The loud voice will make them wonder who you are calling that is so far away.

VII. Thou shalt not proclaim thy doubts.

What they desire is not questions raised, but questions answered. It matters little what you don't believe in; it matters much what you *do* believe in.

VIII. Thou shalt not denounce.

Far better is that wooing note which comes out of a sincere sorrow for the tragedy that has befallen the deceased.

IX. Thou shalt not harp upon one string.

There are many beautiful themes in the symphony of faith. One of these themes is likely to attract you more than others. But you must beware of using it all the time.

X. Thou shalt remember always thy ambassadorship.

You are Christ's representative. Standing in the presence of death, you speak for the Lord of Life. By your presentation of the gospel your Christ will be judged.

Notes

Chapter 1 Preaching for Special Services

1. See Andrew W. Blackwood, "The Demands of Special Occasions," *Pulpit Digest* 35 (Sept. 1954): 65, 68–70, 72–73.

2. Veteran preacher and author Warren W. Wiersbe has this sage advice: "I don't think that pastors and churches necessarily fall from grace if they commemorate special days as long as they focus on Jesus Christ and seek to honor Him. These celebrations are not essential to our salvation; and, if others prefer not to celebrate, so be it. There is room for loving disagreement even among the most devout believers (Gal. 4:10; Rom. 14:1ff.)." See Warren W. Wiersbe, *Preaching and Teaching with Imagination: The Quest for Biblical Ministry* (Wheaton: Victor/SP, 1994), 259.

3. Douglas W. Hix observes that preachers often "prefer not to be relevant" in their weekly preaching schedule but preach through a book of the Bible or the lectionary, ignoring what surrounds them—even their listeners—and not wanting to offend anyone. Preachers who do this end up saying nothing. He writes: "But if we decide that we no longer can justify being silent in the face of these findings, then our work is cut out for us. We must face the corrosive impact of our society's reigning individualism" and address it. See Douglas W. Hix, "Preaching and the Family Crisis," *Journal for Preachers* 17, no. 4 (1994): 9–13.

4. On preaching and worship see Hughes Oliphant Old, *The Reading and Preaching of the Scriptures in the Worship of the Christian Church*, vol. 1, *The Biblical Period* (Grand Rapids: Eerdmans, 1998), especially his statement on p. 7; also Old, *Reading and Preaching*, vol. 2, *The Patristic Age;* R. E. O. White, *A Guide to Preaching: A Practical Primer of Homiletics* (London: Pickering & Inglis, 1973), 3–11; Howard Williams, *My Word: Christian Preaching Today* (London: SCM, 1973), 100.

5. David J. Schlafer, *What Makes This Day Different? Preaching Grace on Special Occasions* (Boston: Cowley, 1998), 5.

6. Carl E. Braaten, *Stewards of the Mysteries* (Minneapolis: Augsburg Fortress, 1983), 10–11.

7. D. W. Cleverley Ford, *Preaching on Special Occasions* (Oxford: Mowbrays, 1975), 1–2.

8. Michael Courtney, "Our Baby Died," *Journal for Preachers* 14, no. 1 (1990): 34.

9. Haddon W. Robinson, *Biblical Preaching: The Development and Delivery of Expository Messages* (Grand Rapids: Baker, 1980). See also Haddon W. Robinson, *Biblical Sermons: How Twelve Preachers Apply the Principles of Biblical Preaching* (Grand Rapids: Baker, 1989) for examples of Robinson's approach to preaching as demonstrated by a variety of practitioners, followed by an analysis and critique by Robinson.

10. For more on Haddon Robinson's perspective on preaching, see Scott M. Gibson, ed., *Making a Difference in Preaching: Haddon W. Robinson on Biblical Preaching* (Grand Rapids: Baker, 1999).

11. See Keith Willhite, "Bullet Versus Buckshot: What Makes the Big Idea Work?" in *The Big Idea of Biblical Preaching: Connecting the Bible to People*, ed. Keith Willhite and Scott M. Gibson (Grand Rapids: Baker, 1998), 13–23; Scott M. Gibson, "Philosophy Versus Method: Big Idea Preaching's Adaptability," in Willhite and Gibson, *Big Idea*, 163–72.

12. Nineteenth-century Dutch theologian J. J. Van Oosterzee supports this approach to preaching. He urges preachers to have a clear idea, which he calls "a short, vigorous *Schlagwort* (pithy sentence) which sticks, which is carried away with them into the great conflict of life, and of which Holy Scripture contains so great a store, whether in the form of or precept of promise." See Van Oosterzee, *Practical Theology: A Manual for Theological Students* (London: Hodder and Stoughton, 1878), 265.

13. Scott M. Gibson, "A Mist in the Pulpit, A Fog in the Pew: Preaching and Clarity," *ABE Journal* 7, no. 3 (Sept. 1999): 11–15.

14. Old, *Reading and Preaching,* 2:352.

15. Eugene H. Peterson, "Introduction," in *Weddings, Funerals, and Special Events,* ed. Eugene H. Peterson, Calvin Miller and others (Carol Steam, Ill: Christianity Today, Inc. and Waco: Word, 1987), 14–15.

16. Søren J. Kierkegaard, *Purity of Heart,* trans. Douglas Steere (New York: Harper & Brothers, 1938), 163ff.; see also Perry H. Biddle, "Back to Tradition—and Beyond," *Christian Ministry* 17, no. 3 (May 1986): 10–11.

Chapter 2 Wedding Sermons

1. Jolene L. and Eugene C. Roehlkepartain, "Why Bother with Personalized Weddings?" *Christian Ministry* 17, no. 3 (May 1986): 15.

2. Ken Williams, "Opening the Door for Unchurched Couples," *Christian Ministry* 17, no. 3 (May 1986): 12.

3. For example, *The Book of Common Prayer* indicates "a homily . . . may follow." See *The Book of Common Prayer* (New York: Seabury Press, 1979), 426. *The Lutheran Agenda* states that the wedding address may be included in the marriage service. Other denominations have liturgies with the sermon included in the ritual; these include The Baptist Union of Great Britain (see *Patterns and Prayers for Christian Worship: A Guidebook for Worship Leaders* [Oxford: Oxford University

Press, 1991], 119–34); the Evangelical Covenant Church [see *The Covenant Book of Worship* (Chicago: Covenant Press, 1981), 143–68]. See also David J. Schlafer, *What Makes This Day Different?* 36.

4. Schlafer, *What Makes This Day Different?* 36.

5. Abraham E. Millgram, *Jewish Worship* (Philadelphia: The Jewish Publication Society of America, 1971), 326–30. There appears to be no marriage liturgy until rabbinical times. See also *The Babylonian Talmud: Seder Nezikin, Baba Bathra II* (London: The Soncino Press, 1935), 621–28.

6. Millgram, *Jewish Worship,* 530–31.

7. Marc Saperstein, *Jewish Preaching 1200–1800: An Anthology* (New Haven: Yale University Press, 1989), 180, 411. Saperstein comments, "At the beginning of the eighteenth century it was lamented that grooms were no longer capable of delivering an appropriate discourse themselves, perhaps an indication that this practice had been the norm" (p. 37). See also Michael Kaufman, *Love, Marriage, and Family in Jewish Law and Tradition* (Northvale, N.J.: Jason Aronson, 1992), 190–92. Jewish marriage rituals had two parts, the betrothal *(Erusin)* and the marriage proper *(Nisuin).* See Millgram, *Jewish Worship,* 327.

8. "The sacramental sign of marriage is the joining of hands, a custom practiced by the Jews (Tobit 7:13), by the Greeks, and by the Romans." See Marion J. Hatchett, *Commentary on the American Prayer Book* (New York: Seabury Press, 1980), 435.

9. Origen, "The First Homily," in *20 Centuries of Great Preaching,* ed. Clyde E. Fant Jr. and William M. Pinson Jr. (Waco: Word Books, 1971), 1:39.

10. For insight on the connection between Greco-Roman marriage rites and Christian marriage rites, see Susan K. Hedahl, *Preaching the Wedding Sermon* (St. Louis: Chalice Press, 1999), 14–21.

11. Ambrose of Milan, "Isaac, or the Soul," in *Seven Exegetical Works,* trans. Michael P. McHugh, vol. 65 of *The Fathers of the Church* (Washington, D.C.: The Catholic University of America Press and Consortium Press, 1972), 36–37. Ambrose interprets the epithalamium in the Song of Songs (3:10–11) as "the love that Christ has toward the daughters of Jerusalem" (p. 37).

12. Paulinus of Nola, "Carmen 25," in David G. Hunter, trans. and ed., *Marriage in the Early Church* (Minneapolis: Augsburg Fortress, 1992), 25, 128–40.

13. See Joseph Martos, *Doors to the Sacred: A Historical Introduction to the Sacraments in the Christian Church* (London: SCM Press, 1981), 400–419.

14. Caesarius of Arles, sermon 42, "A Reproof of Married Men Who Do Not Blush or Fear to Commit Adultery," *Saint Caesarius of Arles Sermons,* vol. 1, trans. Mary Magdeleine Mueller McHugh, in *Fathers of the Church,* 31:213. For orations see sermon 44, "That Chastity Is to Be Observed, Even with One's Own Wife," 222.

15. Martos, *Doors to the Sacred,* 419–26.

16. John Calvin, *Institutes of the Christian Religion,* ed. John T. McNeill, vol. 21 in *The Library of the Christian Classics* (Philadelphia: Westminster Press, 1960), iv.19.34–37; See also Martos, *Doors to the Sacred,* 435–37.

17. Martin Luther, "To the August and Honorable Hans Loser of Pretzsch, Hereditary Marshal of Saxony, My Gracious Lord and Friend," in *Commentary on 1 Corinthians 7,* trans. Edward Sittler, vol. 28 in *Luther's Works,* ed. Hilton C. Oswald (Saint Louis: Concordia, 1973), 3. Luther performed the ceremony in December 1524. See also G. J. Cuming, *A History of Anglican Liturgy* (London: Macmillan, 1969), 17; for "Luther's Marriage Service of 1534," 275–77.

18. John Knox, "The Form of Marriage," in *The Works of John Knox,* ed. David Laing (Edinburgh: James Thin, 1895), 4:198. John Wesley may have preached "A Thought Upon

Marriage" to those preparing to marry. The context is unclear. See "A Thought Upon Marriage," in *Living Thoughts of John Wesley*, ed. James H. Potts (New York: Hune & Eaton, 1891), 400–401.

19. Cuming, *A History of Anglican Liturgy*, 63.

20. Jeremy Taylor, "The Marriage Ring, or, The Mysteriousness and Duties of Marriage" in *Master Sermons through the Ages*, ed. William Alan Sadler Jr. (New York: Harper & Row, 1963), 110–17. The original was much longer. See *The Whole Works of the Right Reverend Jeremy Taylor*, vol. 5 (London: W. Clowes, 1828).

21. W. L., *The Incomparable Jewell. Shewed in a Sermon, London, 1632* (Norwood, N.J.: Walter J. Johnson, Inc., Theatrum Orbis Terrarum, Ltd., 1976).

22. John Donne, "Number 11. Preached at a Mariage [sic]," in *The Sermons of John Donne*, ed. George R. Potter and Evelyn M. Simpson (Berkeley and Los Angeles: University of California Press, 1962), 3:241–55.

23. Horton Davies, *The Worship of the English Puritans* (Glasgow: Dacre Press, 1948), 121.

24. Ibid., 138–39.

25. Cotton Mather, *Ratio Disciplinae Fratrum Nov-Anglorum: A Faithful Account of the Discipline professed and practised in the Churches of New England with Interspersed and Instructive Reflections on the Discipline of the Primitive Churches* (1726; reprint, New York: Arno Press, 1972), 112. See also Horton Davies, *The Worship of the American Puritans, 1629–1730* (New York: Peter Lang, 1990), 187–95.

26. *Transactions of the Baptist Historical Society*, vol. 1 (1908–1909), 122–23. See also Horton Davies, *Worship and Theology in England from Watts and Wesley to Maurice, 1690–1850* (Princeton: Princeton University Press, 1961), 137.

27. Van Oosterzee, *Practical Theology*, 269.

28. Horton Davies, *Worship and Theology in England from Newman to Martineau, 1850–1900* (Princeton: Princeton University Press, 1962), 258.

29. The Anglican liturgy, with its homily, has been the most influential order of service for many denominations. G. J. Cuming notes, "From 1549 onwards, the Marriage service has always been more gently revised than any other" (*History of Anglican Liturgy*, 220).

30. Dietrich Bonhoeffer, "A Wedding Sermon from a Prison Cell," in *Letters and Papers from Prison*, ed. Eberhard Bethge (New York: Macmillan, 1971), 41–47. Bonhoeffer wrote that the best text for a wedding sermon was Romans 15:7, "Accept one another, then, just as Christ accepted you, in order to bring praise to God" (p. 38).

31. Warren W. Wiersbe, *The Dynamics of Preaching* (Grand Rapids: Baker, 1999), 137.

32. J. J. Van Oosterzee says that the purpose of the wedding sermon is to lead "the newly wedded pair to the appreciation of their high privileges, of impressing upon the heart their serious obligations, and of attaching them by the most sacred promises, not only to each other, but also and above all to Him, who must be their third person in the marriage covenant." See Van Oosterzee, *Practical Theology*, 270.

33. Francis C. Rossow, "Toward Wedding Sermons with Substance," *Concordia Journal* 7, no. 1 (January 1981): 9.

34. William Skudlarek, *The Word in Worship: Preaching in a Liturgical Context* (Nashville: Abingdon, 1981), 105.

35. Gwyn Walters lists eight reasons for "an antipathy towards its [wedding sermon's] inclusion." See Gwyn Walters, *Towards Healthy Preaching* (Danvers: privately printed, 1987), 194.

36. Van Oosterzee, *Practical Theology*, 270.

37. See Perry H. Biddle, "Back to Tradition—and Beyond," *Christian Ministry* 17, no. 3 (May 1986): 10–11.

38. Rossow, "Toward Wedding Sermons," 9.

39. My pre-marital sessions are usually six weeks in length or have at least six sessions.

40. Wedding the unchurched is an issue for pastors. The answer to it is beyond the scope of this book. For a discussion on the topic see Douglas Scott, "Should We Wed the Unchurched?" *Leadership* 15, no. 2 (Spring 1994): 98–103.

41. Williams, "Opening the Door," 13. Bracketed statement mine.

42. See Robinson, *Biblical Preaching.* Robinson's stage 6 deals with determining the purpose for a sermon.

43. Douglas J. Rumford, "The Wedding Sermon," in *Leadership Handbooks of Practical Theology,* ed. James D. Berkley (Grand Rapids: Baker, 1992), 1:428.

44. Wiersbe, *The Dynamics of Preaching,* 137.

45. Ibid.

Chapter 3   Funeral Sermons

1. Millgram, *Jewish Worship,* 331.

2. *The Babylonian Talmud: Seder Zera'im, Berakoth* (London: The Soncino Press, 1938), 26–30.

3. Ibid.

4. Millgram, *Jewish Worship,* 332.

5. Marc Saperstein, *Jewish Preaching 1200–1800,* 37.

6. Martin R. P. McGuire, "The Christian Funeral Oration," in *Funeral Orations by Saint Gregory Nazianzen and Saint Ambrose,* vol. 22 ed. Roy Joseph Deferrari, *Fathers of the Church,* vii–viii.

7. Menander, "Treatise II," in *Menander Rhetor,* ed. D. A. Russell and N. G. Wilson (Oxford: Clarendon Press, 1981), 173–79. See also the commentary on pp. 331–36; also "Pseudo-Dionysius," 373–76; and McGuire, "Christian Funeral Oration," x. On Aristotle's use of epideictic speeches and funerals, see James M. Schmitmeyer, *The Words of Worship: Presiding and Preaching at the Rites* (New York: Alba House, 1988), 118–20.

8. McGuire, "Christian Funeral Oration," ix–x.

9. Ibid., xvi. McGuire observes that Nazianzen's oration on St. Basil "is really an *epitaphios logos,* but one in which the orator has made important modifications, from the viewpoint of the traditional form, in content, *topoi,* and emphasis to suit his purpose. The pagan funeral oration is here transformed into a masterpiece of Christian eloquence in which the pagan elements do not assume undue importance, but are harmoniously subordinated to Christian use" (p. xviii).

10. Ibid. Some scholars suggest that during the liturgical celebration, funeral sermons did not take place. However, there is also indication that Ambrose preached at the Mass of his brother. See John Allyn Melloh, "Homily or Eulogy? The Dilemma of Funeral Preaching," *Worship* 67 (1993): 502–18. Also see Ambrose of Milan, "On His Brother Satyrus," trans. John J. Sullivan and Martin R. P. McGuire in McGuire, "Christian Funeral Oration," 159–97.

11. McGuire, "Christian Funeral Oration," xix.

12. Robert G. Hughes, "Why I Preach at Funerals," *Journal for Preachers* 9, no. 2 (1986): 8.

13. Tony Walter, *Funerals and How to Improve Them* (London: Hodder & Stoughton, 1990), 94.

14. Hughes, "Why I Preach at Funerals," 9.

15. Davies, *Worship of the English Puritans,* 45.

16. Harry S. Stout, *The New England Soul: Preaching and Religious Culture in Colonial New England* (New York: Oxford University Press, 1986), 122–23.

17. Davies, *Worship of the American Puritans,* 197–98.

18. Cotton Mather, *Ratio Disciplinae,* 117. Customs varied among New England Puritans and Separatists. The Separatists frowned on any ceremony—prayers, Scripture reading, or preaching. First-generation Puritans likewise buried the body without ceremony. See Davies, *Worship of the American Puritans,* 195–96.

19. Davies, *Worship of the English Puritans,* 45–46.

20. John Donne, "Number 10. Preached at the funerals of Sir William Cokayne Knight, Alderman of London, December 12, 1626," in *The Sermons of John Donne*, ed. Evelyn M. Simpson and George R. Potter (Berkeley and Los Angeles: University of California Press, 1954), 7:257–78.

21. Jonathan Crowther, *A True and Complete Portraiture of Methodism* (New York: J. Eastburn, 1813), 226.

22. Davies, *Worship and Theology in England: 1690–1850,* 136.

23. See for example Edward T. Hiscox, *The Star Book for Ministers* (Valley Forge: Judson Press, 1968), 185. This edition is a reprint of Hiscox's late-nineteenth-century service book and is a good example of the resources for pastors in the period. Hiscox (1814–1901) suggests funeral addresses contain "remarks which the peculiar circumstances of each case may call forth, [and] it is desireable that they should address some instruction to those present, other than the relatives; some of whom seldom attend any other religious services."

24. For example, see Benjamin Wadsworth, *A Discourse Delivered November 19, A.D. 1820, on account of the Late Death of Bethiah Shelden, Nov. 3, at age 24 and of Benjamin Hezekiah Flint, Nov. 9, in the 17th year of his age* (Andover: Flagg and Gould, 1821); Heman Dyer, *An Address Delivered in the Chapel of the University, Saturday, May 29, 1847, on the occasion of the interment of The Remains of the Late Prof. Stone* (Pittsburgh: George Parkin & Co., 1847); Jacob Merrill Manning, *Sermons and Addresses* (Boston and New York: Houghton, Mifflin and Company, 1889), 532–42.

25. Ozora S. Davis, *Preaching on Church and Community Occasions* (Chicago: University of Chicago, 1928), 202. Edgar N. Jackson also makes the same point for other periods during the century. See Edgar N. Jackson, *The Christian Funeral: Its Meaning, Its Purpose, and Its Modern Practice* (New York: Channel Press, 1966).

26. Thomas G. Long, "The Funeral: Changing Patterns and Teachable Moments," *Journal for Preachers* 19, no. 3 (Easter 1996): 7.

27. Ibid.

28. The literature is extensive. For example, see Reginald H. Fuller, "Lectionary for Funerals," *Worship* 56 (Jan. 1982): 36–63; Robert A. Krieg, "The Funeral Homily: A Theological View," *Worship* 58 (May 1984): 222–39; Lawrence E. Mick, "Celebrating Funerals in the United States," in *The Funeral Book for Homilist and Presiders,* ed. Eltin Griffin (Mystic, Conn.: Twenty-Third Publications, 2000), 20–35.

29. Mark E. Chapman, "The Authentic Word in the Face of Death: Reflections on Preaching at Funerals," *Currents in Theology & Mission* 22 (1995): 39.

30. Thomas H. Seig, "Preaching at Funerals: Homily or Eulogy?" *The Priest* 40 (January 1984): 42. For a similar Catholic view, see Eltin Griffin, "Funerals and Evangelization" in Griffin, *Funeral Book,* 36–39.

31. For a helpful discussion on theology and the funeral, see Paul Waitman Hoon, "Theology, Death, and the Funeral Liturgy," *Union Seminary Quarterly Review* 31, no. 3 (spring 1976): 169–81.

32. Van Oosterzee, *Practical Theology,* 275.

33. Jackson, *The Christian Funeral,* 31.

34. Roger Van Harn, "Only the Gospel Will Do," *Reformed Worship* 24 (June 1992): 8.

35. Long, "The Funeral: Changing Patterns," 8.

36. Chapman, "The Authentic Word," 42.

37. See for example William R. Baird Sr. and John E. Baird, *Funeral Meditations* (Nashville: Abingdon, 1966), 11; Griffin, *Funeral Book,* 28–29; Paul E. Irion, *The Funeral and the Mourners: Pastoral Care of the Bereaved* (New York and Nashville: Abingdon, 1954), 104; Dan S. Lloyd, *Leading Today's Funerals: A Pastoral Guide for Improving Bereavement*

Ministry (Grand Rapids: Baker, 1997), 22; Van Harn, "Only the Gospel," 8.

38. Tony Walter, *Funerals and How to Improve Them,* 95.

39. For example, *The Book of Common Prayer* indicates "A homily may be preached" (p. 480).

40. Quoted in Davis, *Preaching on Church and Community Occasions,* 202.

41. Alvin C. Rueter, *Making Good Preaching Better: A Step-by-Step Guide to Scripture-based, People-Centered Preaching* (Collegeville, Minn.: The Liturgical Press, 1997), 181.

42. See Robert D. Firebaugh, "Whose Funeral Is It, Anyway?" *Ministry* 60:9 (Sept. 1987): 18–19.

43. I found it helpful to keep a small file on the families of the church. The information was placed on three-by-five-inch cards. After each visit I wrote down information about family members, prayer concerns, hobbies and interests, and whatever else might be helpful to me as I got to know them. The information was invaluable later.

44. Andrew W. Blackwood, *The Funeral: A Source Book for Ministers* (Philadelphia: Westminster, 1942), 136.

45. Bryan Chapell, *Christ-Centered Preaching: Redeeming the Expository Sermon* (Grand Rapids: Baker, 1994), 346.

46. Wiersbe, *The Dynamics of Preaching,* 135.

47. See John S. Mansell, *The Funeral* (Nashville: Abingdon, 1998), 35. Others argue the same point. See Roger F. Miller, "Handling the Hard Cases," in Peterson, Miller, and others, *Weddings, Funerals, and Special Events,* 127.

48. Griffin, "Funerals and Evangelization," 38.

49. Melloh, "Homily or Eulogy," 516, n. 66.

50. For example, see Scott M. Gibson, *A. J. Gordon: American Premillennialist* (Lanham, Md.: University Press of America, 2001), 212. Boston Baptist A. J. Gordon's funeral had five sermons preached totalling several hours.

51. Calvin Ratz, "Funeral and Graveside Services," in Peterson, Miller, and others, *Weddings, Funerals, and Special Events*, 104.

52. Blackwood, 137; Baird and Baird, *Funeral Meditations*, 10–11. Some, like Desmond Forristal, suggest that the funeral sermon should be no longer than five minutes. See Desmond Forristal, "Parish Practicalities," in Griffin, *Funeral Book*, 31–33; Edgar N. Jackson advises that a funeral sermon be brief, about "six or seven minutes" (*The Christian Funeral*, 42); Dan S. Lloyd suggests that a service ought to last no longer than twenty minutes (*Leading Today's Funeral*, 50); Calvin Ratz recommends ten- to twelve-minute sermons ("Funeral and Graveside Services," 104). Warren Wiersbe recommends, "Limit the service to about thirty minutes, and shorter if possible" (*The Dynamics of Preaching*, 136).

53. Blackwood, *The Funeral*, 140–41.

54. Ratz, "Funeral and Graveside Services," 104.

55. Wiersbe, *The Dynamics of Preaching*, 136.

56. Ibid., 135.

57. Earl Daniels, *The Funeral Message* (Nashville: Cokesbury, 1937).

58. Ibid., 32–33. Thomas G. Long suggests eight themes for funeral preaching: kerygmatic, ecclesial, oblational, eucharistic, therapeutic, commemorative, missional, and educational. See Thomas G. Long, "Telling the Truth about Death and Life: Preaching at Funerals," *Journal for Preachers* 20, no. 3 (Easter 1997): 3–12. Long acknowledges his debt to Hoon. See also Hoon, "Theology, Death," 174–81.

59. Mark Coppenger, "Services for People You Barely Know," in Peterson, Miller, and others, *Weddings, Funerals, and Special Events*, 113.

60. Daniels, *Funeral Message*, 35–51. See also Firebaugh, "Whose Funeral Is It, Anyway?" 18–19.

61. See Kenn Filkins, "Funeral for a Funny Lady: Humor and the Funeral Message," *Preaching* 9 (Jan.–Feb. 1994): 25–26.

62. Mansell, *The Funeral,* 37.

63. Thomas F. Backer, "Doorkeeper for Christ: Funeral Service for Gene Salter," Omaha, Neb., 19 May 1998.

64. Thomas V. Haugen, "2 Timothy 4:6–8," sermon for Preaching for Special Occasions, Gordon-Conwell Theological Seminary, 20 Oct. 1998.

65. Long, "The Funeral: Changing Patterns," 8.

66. Daniels, *Funeral Message,* 52–68.

67. Roger F. Miller, in Peterson, Miller, and others, *Weddings, Funerals, and Special Events,* 128.

68. Daniels, *Funeral Message,* 70–89.

69. Bryan Wilkerson, "A Purpose Runs through It," *Preaching Today* 133, n.d.

70. This angle is suggested in Barbara G. Schmitz, *The Life of Christ and the Death of a Loved One: Crafting the Funeral Homily* (Lima, Ohio: CSS Publishing, 1995), 17–23.

71. Davis, *Preaching on Church and Community Occasions,* 204.

72. R. Earl Allen, *Memorial Messages* (Nashville: Broadman, 1964), 7.

73. Wesley Carr, *Brief Encounters: Pastoral Ministry through Baptisms, Weddings, and Funerals* (London: SPCK, 1994), 121.

74. Robert Blair, *The Minister's Funeral Handbook* (Grand Rapids: Baker, 1990), 11.

75. Stuart Briscoe, "The Funeral Sermon," in Berkley, *Leadership Handbooks,* 1:477.

Chapter 4 Baptism and Infant Presentation Sermons

1. Old, *Reading and Preaching,* 1:180.

2. Ibid., 1:272.

3. William Telfer, *Cyril of Jerusalem and Nemesius of Emesa* (Philadelphia: Westminster, 1955), 31.

4. Old, *Reading and Preaching,* 2:318–19. For a descriptive account of Augustine and baptismal sermons, see F. Van Der Meer, *Augustine the Bishop,* trans. Brian Battershaw and G. R. Lamb (London and New York: Sheed and Ward), 361–79.

5. Old, *Reading and Preaching,* 2:320. In light of this, Old comments about Cyril of Jerusalem's response to Hellenistic mystery religions: "When Cyril first preached his catechetical sermons the making of the vows was for him, obviously, the center of attention, but as he began to think of the sacraments as mysteries and catechetical preaching as mystagogy, and as his converts had already been baptized, another understanding of baptism and therefore catechetical preaching came into play" (2:22).

"These auxiliary rites of baptism [exorcised oil, removal of clothes] multiplied greatly under the influence of the Hellenistic mystery religions, and it is through these same auxiliary rites that a good number of alien attitudes developed around the sacraments. They all fed on the basic idea that religious ceremonial which was seen with the eyes and experienced with the senses communicated better than the reading and preaching of Scripture" (2:23).

"He [Cyril] firmly believed in salvation by ceremony, just as the adherents of the Greek mystery religions did" (2:25).

6. Ibid., 2:198. Regarding John Chrysostom, Old comments, "What immediately strikes us about John Chrysostom's catechetical preaching is that it shows far greater interest in moral catechism than in either doctrinal or liturgical catechism" (2:198).

7. Ibid., 2:398.

8. Ibid., 2:412. Old observes, "With this transition to infant baptism the penitential disciplines of Lent would have lost their significance had not the threat of barbarian invasion, at this same time, imbued them with new importance. After all, one could hardly ask infants to fast for forty days. On the

other hand, Christians saw in the threat of barbarian invasion a reason to intensify their self-examination and the disciplines of penitential prayer" (2:412).

9. See Arthur G. Patzia, "Baby Dedication in the Believers' Church," *American Baptist Quarterly* 3, no. 1 (March 1984): 64.

10. Hughes Oliphant Old, *The Shaping of the Reformed Baptismal Rite in the Sixteenth Century* (Grand Rapids: Eerdmans, 1992), 59. See also Hughes Oliphant Old, "Worship: That Is Reformed According to Scripture," in *Guides to the Reformed Tradition,* ed. John H. Leith and John W. Kuykendall (Atlanta: John Knox, 1984), 16.

11. Old, *Shaping,* 61.

12. Ibid., 59.

13. Ibid., 68–69.

14. George H. Williams, *The Radical Reformation,* 3rd ed., vol. 15 of *Sixteenth-Century Essays & Studies* (Kirksville, Mo.: Sixteenth-Century Journal Publishers, 1992), 230.

15. Quoted in Davies, *English Puritans,* 45.

16. W. M. S. West, "The Child and the Church: A Baptist Perspective," in *Pilgrim Pathways: Essays in Baptist History in Honor of B. R. White,* ed. William H. Brackney and Paul S. Fiddes with John H. Y. Briggs (Macon: Mercer University Press, 1999), 78.

17. Michael J. Walker, "The Relation of Infants to Church, Baptism and Gospel in Seventeenth-Century Baptist Theology," *Baptist Quarterly* 21, no. 6 (April 1966): 242–62. See especially pp. 250 and 258. See also West, "Child and Church," 79–80.

18. Quoted in Keith Wimmersberger, "Infant Dedication: A Rite of Community Renewal for Baptist Congregations," *Foundations* 20, no. 3 (July-Sept. 1977): 245–48. See also Morgan Edwards, *Customs of the Primitive Churches* (1774).

19. Robert Robinson, *A History of Baptism,* ed. David Benedict (Boston: Lincoln & Edmands, 1817), 490–93.

20. Davies, *Worship and Theology in England: 1690–1850*, 132.

21. Jonathan Crowther, *A True and Complete Portraiture of Methodism*, 226.

22. Cotton Mather, *Ratio Disciplinae*, 76.

23. Charles E. Bateman, *John Clifford: Free Church Leader and Preacher* (London: National Council of the Evangelical Free Churches, 1904), 77.

24. Russell H. Conwell, "Form of Service Used in Ceremony of Dedicating Infants," in Agnes Rush Burr, *Russell H. Conwell and His Work* (Philadelphia: John C. Winston, 1926), 339–402.

25. *Companion to the Book of Services: Introduction, Commentary, and Instructions for Using the New United Methodist Services* (Nashville: Abingdon, 1988), 84.

26. See Bonhoeffer, *Letters and Papers*, 291, 294–300.

27. See Calvin, *Institutes*, 4.14.1–3; Louis Berkof defines sacrament thus: "A sacrament is a holy ordinance instituted by Christ, in which by sensible signs the grace of God in Christ, and the benefits of the covenant of grace, are represented, sealed, and applied to believers, and these, in turn, give expression to their faith and allegiance to God." He adds, "As signs and seals they are means of grace, that is, means of strengthening the inward grace that is wrought in the heart by the Holy Spirit." Louis Berkhof, *Systematic Theology* (Grand Rapids: Eerdmans, 1939), 617–18.

28. Robert M. Shelton, "Baptism and Proclamation," *Reformed Liturgy and Music* 22 (winter 1988): 8.

29. Berkhof, *Systematic Theology*, 616. See also Millard J. Erickson, *Christian Theology* (Grand Rapids: Baker, 1985), 1011.

30. Calvin, *Institutes*, 4.14.4.

31. Ibid.

32. My understanding of infant presentation or parental dedication (I use the terms interchangeably) is that as the par-

ents present their infant to the Lord in front of the believing congregation, they are dedicating themselves to raise the child in a Christian way of life, the congregation bearing witness to their act of dedication. The burden rests on the parents as they commit themselves to nurture their son or daughter in the name of Christ.

33. Patzia, "Baby Dedication," 64.

34. Arthur G. Patzia comments, "In order to justify this ceremony, appeal is made to (1) the examples of dedication in the Bible, (2) Jesus blessing the children, and (3) various biblical attitudes and admonitions to train and nurture children in the Lord" ("Baby Dedication," 66); He further remarks, "Dedication is not a 'sealing' or a 'sign' of the covenant; nor is it a dry 'sacrament.' Among other things, baptism in the Believers' church is a Believers' baptism; it is a rite which belongs to one's spiritual and not physical birth; it is a decisive act and does not await its completion in a subsequent rite such as confirmation. The true meaning of baptism is lived out in the ethical life of each Christian (Rom 6:1–11; Col. 3:1–3)" (ibid., 72). See also R. W. Rusling, "The Status of Children," *Baptist Quarterly* 18, no. 6 (1959–1969): 245–57.

35. Garth Bolinger, "Infant Rites," *Leadership* 8, no. 4 (fall 1987): 121.

36. Melissa Buono, "Romans 6:1–11," sermon for Preaching for Special Occasions, Gordon-Conwell Theological Seminary, 22 Sept. 1998.

37. Susan Gleason, "Romans 8:26–27," sermon for Preaching for Special Occasions, Gordon-Conwell Theological Seminary, 22 Sept. 1998.

Chapter 5   Preaching at the Celebration of the Lord's Supper

1. Isaac Levy, *A Guide to Passover* (London: Jewish Chronicle Publications, 1958), 58.

2. See Deut. 6:20–33; *The Babylonian Talmud: Sedar Mo'ed, Pesahim* (London: The Soncino Press, 1938), 593–95.

3. Millgram, *Jewish Worship*, 301–2.

4. Ibid., 309.

5. Saperstein, *Jewish Preaching*, 32.

6. For a sample sermon see ibid., 361–73, "Sermon for the Sabbath Preceding Passover" (1782, Prague).

7. William Rosenau, ed., *Seder Hagadah Home Service for Passover Eve* (New York: Bloch Publishing, 1916); Eric-Peter Lipson, *Passover Haggadah: A Messianic Celebration* (San Francisco: JFJ Publishing, 1986).

8. *The Didache*, trans. James A. Kleist, vol. 6 of *Ancient Christian Writers* (Westminster, Md.: The Newman Press, 1961), 9, 10, 14; Old, *Reading and Preaching*, 1:292–94. Although the Didache does not mention preaching, Old observes, "Somewhat indirectly, yet nevertheless quite clearly, the Didache gives us a picture of a vigorous and varied ministry of the Word" (p. 256).

9. Cyril C. Richardson, *Early Christian Fathers* (New York: Macmillan, 1970), 25.

10. Justin Martyr, "The First Apology of Justin, the Martyr," in *Early Christian Fathers*, 287.

11. Old, *Reading and Preaching*, 2:194, 230–31, 320–21, 356.

12. Ibid., 2:256–57. See also Augustine's *Sermons in John*, Sermon 25.

13. Bard Thompson, ed., *Liturgies of the Western Church* (Philadelphia: Fortress Press, 1961), 27–34.

14. Ibid., 45.

15. Old, *Reading and Preaching*, 3:394–98.

16. Ibid., 3:454–56.

17. Martin Luther, "The German Mass and Order of Service" (1526), in *Liturgies of the Western Church*, 126.

18. Ibid., 129–30.

19. Martin Bucer, "Psalter with Complete Church Practice, Strassburg, 1539: Concerning the Lord's Supper, or Mass, and the Sermons," in *Early Christian Fathers*, 171. See also

"The Lord's Supper at Strasbourg, 1524," in Cuming, *History of Anglican Liturgy*, 278.

20. John Calvin, "The Form of Church Prayers and Hymns with the Manner of Administrating the Sacraments and Consecrating Marriage According to the Custom of the Ancient Church," (Strassburg 1545 and Geneva 1542), in *Liturgies of the Western Church*, 204.

21. John Knox, *The Form of Prayers and Ministrations of the Sacraments, Used in the English Congregation at Geneva, 1556,* in Laing, *John Knox*, 192.

22. *Transactions of the Congregational Historical Society*, London, 6:334. Quoted in Davies, *Worship and Theology in England: 1690–1850*, 102.

23. Cotton Mather, *Ratio Disciplinea*, 96. See also Davies, *American Puritans*, 163–86.

24. Crowther, *A True and Complete Portraiture of Methodism*, 242–43. Methodists received the Supper infrequently because the number of Anglican priests who sympathized with them was small. Eventually they celebrated their own version of the Supper in their chapels. See Davies, *Worship and Theology in England: 1690–1850*, 200–1, 207–9. See also Potts, *Living Thoughts of John Wesley*, 19–22.

25. Crowther, *A True and Complete Portraiture of Methodism*, 226. See for example John Wesley's "Means of Grace," in *John Wesley's Sermons: An Anthology*, ed. Albert C. Outler and Richard P. Heitzenrater (Nashville: Abingdon, 1991), 158–71.

26. Davies, *Worship and Theology in England: 1850–1900*, 139–43.

27. Ibid., 148–49.

28. F. Roy Coad, *History of the Brethren Movement* (Grand Rapids: Eerdmans, 1968), 205, 269, 274.

29. J. N. Darby, "The Brethren, Their Doctrines, Etc.," in H. A. Ironside, *A Historical Sketch of the Brethren Movement* (Grand Rapids: Zondervan, 1942), 194.

30. See for example Charles Haddon Spurgeon, "The Right Observance of the Lord's Supper," *C. H. Spurgeon's Sermons for Special Occasions*, ed. Charles T. Cook (London: Marshall, Morgan & Scott, 1958), 246–56.

31. Marion J. Hatchett, *Commentary on the American Prayer Book* (New York: Seabury Press, 1981), 332.

32. *Companion to the Book of Services*, 55.

33. William Willimon, "Planning the Lord's Supper," in *Leadership Handbooks*, 1:351.

34. Davis, *Preaching on Church and Community Occasions*, 210.

35. See also Howard G. Hageman, *Pulpit and Table: Some Chapters in the History of Worship in the Reformed Churches* (Richmond: John Knox Press, 1962), 113–20.

36. Calvin, *Institutes*, 4.17.39.

37. Willimon, "Planning the Lord's Supper," 352.

38. David L. Larsen, *The Anatomy of Preaching: Identifying the Issues in Preaching Today* (Grand Rapids: Kregel, 1989), 123.

39. Craig Brian Larson, "The Crux of Communion," in *Changing Lives through Preaching and Worship*, ed. Marshall Shelley (Nashville: Moorings, 1995), 273.

40. Willimon, "Planning the Lord's Supper," 351.

41. Larson, "Crux of Communion," 271.

42. Susan Gleason, "Luke 24:13–35," sermon for Preaching for Special Occasions, Gordon-Conwell Theological Seminary, 3 November 1998.

43. Melissa Buono, "Luke 7:36–50," sermon for Preaching for Special Occasions, Gordon-Conwell Theological Seminary, 3 November 1998.

Chapter 6   Speaking on Other Occasions

1. See for example Cook, *C. H. Spurgeon's Sermons for Special Occasions*.

2. Wiersbe, *The Dynamics of Preaching*, 134.

3. Menander, "Pseudo-Dionysius," 373.

4. Duane Litfin, *Public Speaking: A Handbook for Christians,* 2nd ed. (Grand Rapids: Baker, 1992), 82.

5. Ibid.

6. See also Robinson, *Biblical Preaching,* 31–45.

7. Gibson, *Making a Difference,* 101.

8. Wiersbe, *The Dynamics of Preaching,* 134.

9. Myron Augsburger, "Rethinking the Evangelistic Sermon," *Leadership* 11:3 (summer 1990): 63.

10. For an interesting discussion on evangelism and evangelistic preaching, see Craig A. Loscalzo, "How Are They to Hear? Evangelism and Proclamation," *Review and Expositor* 90 (1993): 103–13.

11. William D. Thompson, "Evangelism from the Pulpit," *Preaching for Decision* (Valley Forge: Office of Evangelism, National Ministries, American Baptist Churches in the U.S.A.), 1.

12. Robert E. Coleman, "Preparing and Delivering an Evangelistic Message," in *The Calling of an Evangelist,* ed. J. Douglas (Minneapolis: World Wide Publications, 1987), 178.

13. Chapell, *Christ-Centered Preaching,* 348.

14. Wilbur D. Nesbit, *After-Dinner Speeches and How to Make Them* (Chicago and New York: Reilly & Lee, 1927), 24–29.

15. Ibid., 24.

16. Thomas V. Haugen, after-dinner speech, Preaching for Special Occasions, Gordon-Conwell Theological Seminary, 1 Dec. 1998.

17. Chevis F. Horne, "Using Community Opportunities for Proclamation," *Church Administration* 18, no. 10 (July 1976): 38.

18. Cal LeMon, "Speaking Before the Community," in Peterson, Miller, and others, *Weddings, Funerals, and Special Events,* 170.

19. James D. Berkley, "Baccalaureate Services," in Berkley, *Leadership Handbooks,* 232–33.

20. Ibid., 233.

21. Frederick D. Kershner, *Sermons for Special Days* (New York: George H. Doran Co., 1922), 150.

22. H. W. Reed, *Baccalaureate Messages* (Grand Rapids: Baker, 1960), 24.

23. "You Bet It's Over," *The Chronicle of Higher Education* 2 June 2000: A12, 14.

24. Jack Sanford, "Memo to Commencement Speakers," *Christianity Today* 8 (May 1970): 14.

25. Davis, *Preaching on Church and Community Occasions,* 137.

Scott M. Gibson is Assistant Dean and Associate Professor of Preaching and Ministry at Gordon-Conwell Theological Seminary, South Hamilton, Massachusetts, where he teaches homiletics. He earned the master of divinity degree from Gordon-Conwell, the master of theology degree in homiletics from Princeton Theological Seminary, the master of theology degree in church history from the University of Toronto, and the doctor of philosophy degree in church history from the University of Oxford.